Sassy & Saved

*One woman's journey to finding
purpose beyond the pain.*

Aimee P. Miller

First printing: 2020 aimeepmiller.com

References: McClain-Walters, Michelle: The Esther Anointing, 2014. Published by Charisma House, Charisma Media/ Charisma House Book Group.

ISBN: 978-1-09831-626-6 (print)
ISBN: 978-1-09831-627-3 (ebook)

I dedicate this book to the woman finding herself again in Jesus

Confront your fears and limitations head on. Find your voice and remain rooted in the unfailing love God has for you. You have the power to be set free fully and completely. There is purpose beyond the pain. I am a Sassy and Saved woman who found her path to freedom and purpose beyond the pain.

"Now the Lord is the spirit, and where the Spirit of the Lord is, there is freedom."

(2 Corinthians 3:17)

You are loved; you are accepted, forgiven and freed to live for him.

Contents

ENDORSEMENTS

"Aimee shares her vulnerable path to freedom for modern women and is carrier of the freedom that she has personally experienced. She bares all with refreshing wisdom, wry humor, no-nonsense faith, liberating insight through biblical stories, and fearless sassy honesty that will have you laughing and crying. Sassy & Saved marries experiential wisdom with the Word of God to encourage others to remain immovably rooted in the unfailing love of God."

Elizabeth Grisham
Author, Speaker, Host of the Signature Podcast
Founder of Signature Wo.

-

"There's a deep place of vulnerability and authenticity that lures in the reader through humor, raw emotions, and spiritual truths. No matter how unqualified you feel, you're left inspired that God can move through even the darkest seasons of your life for a greater purpose. Aimee finds purpose through the pain while trekking on the journey to spiritual freedom. She has shown that with the Father's strength, courage and hope are sure to follow. There's true power in our testimony."

Maegan Pittman
Lead Pastor of Celebration Church Orlando

-

"An invaluable, heartfelt, spiritual insight that will both encourage and excite the reader. This affirming message of spiritual freedom must be read and treasured."

Heather Lindsey,
Speaker and author of Silent Seasons
Founder of the Pinky Promise

-

"Sassy and Saved takes you on a journey of emotions I would describe as vulnerable, authentic and ultimately redeemed! Aimee unfolds the raw moments of her life while revealing how God's redemptive grace and love was in sync with her every move. She unpacks tragedy in a clear and practical way giving hope to every woman who asks, "Am I too flawed to be used by God"? Aimee's book, but ultimately her life, is an inspiring, power-filled, passionate, & resounding "YES" to every woman who looks around for that answer!"

Jessica Huffman Co-Founder and Pastor
at Pneuma Life Church
Founder of #GirlGang Women's Movement

-

"This book carries a living word for each of us. Through her wisdom and life experiences, Aimee reveals divine insights that bring understanding to spiritual freedom, clarity to our identity, and purpose beyond the pain."

Sara L. Evans,
Founder and Senior Leader of Inspire

-

"Aimee P. Miller is an absolute gem. She is a very gifted writer. Her insights, experiences, and stories, laced with fabulous humor, sassiness, and straight up honesty, will have the reader very engaged. Sassy & Saved is packed with wisdom and practical application of truths to help each of us succeed in life of healing from trauma and pain. Here Aimee leads us into profound yet practical truths that inspire a heart of absolute trust in a good and perfect Father who always ensures our victory. I believe this book will become a source of encouragement and insight for countless numbers of people."

Eric Banfield,
Founder and Senior Pastor
of Grace Church

-

INTRODUCTION

IF YOU WOULD HAVE TOLD ME FIFTEEN YEARS AGO I would be saved and working on a book about my Christian walk, I would have laughed. And so the story goes, right? God has a way of redefining our expectations. He takes the most broken things and makes them the most beautiful things. Many of us have faced painful situations throughout our lives. I want to tell you about a woman who faced verbal, mental and physical abuse and rejection, unsuccessful relationships; it was during one of the lowest points of my life of being lost when I realized I had to make a decision to change my situation. Fourteen years ago I gave my heart to Jesus, and still found myself broken. I want to tell you how I overcame depression, fear, low self-esteem, and negativity by refusing to become bound to those things which held me captive for years. Being a wife and a mother I had determined it was time to find purpose beyond my pain and step into who God called me to be. Determination and persistence helped me find freedom. No matter what you've endured in the past, there's a purpose for your life.

There's no situation too difficult or pain too hard that God can't handle. Little did I know that I was about to unravel. I was about to be in such a crucial season, a season that would change my life forever. I was serving in my church, I was doing everything I needed to do, and I was playing all the parts. But I still felt like something was missing. I could preach it, I could speak it, I could give all the girlfriend advice, pray over you, but I didn't feel it. I looked like the "perfect church member" I tithed, volunteered and served. Little did I know that I didn't fall apart alone. Jesus was right there all along waiting for my pivotal unravel. The layers of defense walls I put up and built so well disintegrated like sand in the wind. I was emotionally bare. I was in the shower, face down, crying, begging, screaming, that if this is what life is like I don't want it. I remember saying, "God, if this is what I deserve because of my sin, my bad choices, free-will, I cannot do this, I have lived in so much heart ache my entire life, I'm tired of being strong, tired of always gritting it through. I am tired of fighting, you hear me! I am done." I cried for so long what seemed like hours, the bathroom completely fogged up, and the hot water all gone. Ice cold water from the showerhead piercing my skin, it was so uncomfortable but what was more devastating is that I didn't care. I was so tired of being devastated. God never left me, He never walked away. I probably would have walked away at myself. He softly and so lightly spoke to me like a newborn baby. He led me and steadily walked with me through healing and completeness to finding purpose beyond my pain.

God said, "Aimee, get up." I cried, begged and pleaded that I didn't want to get up. I was empty, blank, emotionally, physically, spiritually devastated, not worth it. I couldn't put up with the abuse, hatred and manipulation anymore. God said it again so softly but clearly, there was no mistaking his voice. "Get up, I am with you, you are not alone." So I got up, got dressed, and looked in the mirror. My face red, swollen eyes, pink nose, congested, wet tangled up hair. I stared into my blood shot eyes, wiped my hands across the fogged mirror, and said to myself, "I am alone now, where are you now God?" I laughed at the thought, I am losing it, and I am talking to myself in the mirror. I didn't hear anything. I have always been sassy; it has got me in trouble a lot and sometimes makes for a good comedian.

I remember walking outside in the backyard, asking the children what would they like for dinner, and God said, "I never left." How many times have you heard people say listen for Gods voice and guidance, or out of scriptural context. It's used in the churches, journals, Bible studies, and church groups. I couldn't hear Gods voice before because I was too busy listening to mine. There was no earth shaking, light from the sky moment. It was a very vivid, deep, confident voice. I believe there are two things you can choose to believe. There is truth and there are facts. The fact is I had so much pain in my past. The fact was that my reality hurt so bad I couldn't do it anymore. I lost myself to all the negative facts. I became so consciously emerged by the doubt, fear and insecurity from years of abuse from really bad relationships and childhood that I entangled the truth and the facts. I couldn't differentiate the two. The truth is God is the only way, the Truth and the life.

The darkness has not overcome it. Means the darkness of evil never has and never will overcome or extinguish Gods light. You have purpose beyond the pain. God is in you and lives through you; you can choose to believe the facts in your life or the truth over your life. When we follow Jesus, the true light, the "Truth," we can avoid walking blindly. That voice of doubt that tries to bind you from finding your purpose. Scripture tells us He lights the path ahead of us so we can see how to live. He removes the darkness of sin from our lives. In what ways have you allowed the light of Christ to shine in your life? Although I stumbled and was living in darkness, there was a light, we all have. It is in mankind, planted, growing, destined. Light always wins. Jesus is the creator and sustainer of all things and the source of eternal life. This is THE TRUTH. The truth about Jesus and the foundation of all truth. If we cannot or do not believe the basic truth, we will not have enough faith to trust our enteral destiny to him, our purpose beyond the pain.

"In him was life, and that life was the light of all mankind. The light shines in the darkness and the darkness has not overcome it." (John 1: 4-5 NIV). Once we digest and adjust ourselves with His truth, then we will be filled with it and the truth of His unfailing complete goodness, love and salvation that saved us from the penalty of sin and death (John 3:16-17). God's love is not static or self-centered; it reaches out and draws others in.

God has set the pattern of true love, the truest of love. This book is about the journey of one woman finding purpose beyond the pain. Your past doesn't define who you are. I am Sassy and Saved. I wanted to write this book for women who have been affected by emotional, physical and mental abuse. The mission of the book is to empower, inspire and encourage women to forgive themselves and those who have hurt you, and transform into the woman God called you to be. I believe a Godly woman who lives with passion, purpose and walks in boldness is free and no longer bound by the shame, guilt and doubt that once bounded you. I challenge you to step up and step out and become all God called you to be. ... Qualified & Called. It's time for you to be the woman God created you to be. God is telling you. He is whispering to you. There is a calling on your life, there is a transformation waiting to begin. Are you ready to walk? There is a shift about to happen in your life. I am praying for you. Before we start, I want to pray a few prayers over you. The first is found in Luke 8:16-17.

> "No one lights a lamp and hides it in a clay jar or puts it under a bed. Instead, they put it on a stand, so that those who come in can see the light. For there is nothing hidden that will not be disclosed, and nothing concealed that will not be known or brought out into the open."

God doesn't want you to hide your light. Let it shine. Shine that light, to help others. Your testimony should be shared with others. God knows every detail, every life event, and here's a secret. He doesn't care, He loves you, all of you no matter what. Here's another secret, no matter how much of a mess you think you made, you didn't mess up his plan, because you're not that powerful.

You have a purpose in your life. Look to this scripture planted in Ephesians 3:14-20, it's of spiritual growth. It was written by Paul, and Paul wrote Ephesians to strengthen the believers in Ephesus with spiritual growth. He explained the nature and purpose of the church and the body of Christ.

> "For this reason I kneel before the Father, from whom every family in heaven and on earth derives its name. I pray that out of his glorious riches he may strengthen you with power through his spirit in your inner being, so that Christ may dwell in your hearts through faith. And I pray that you, being rooted and established in love, may have power, together with all the Lord's holy people, to grasp how wide and long and high and deep is the love of Christ, and to know this love that surpasses knowledge – that you may be filled to the measure of all the fullness of God."

(Ephesians 3:14-20)

God's love is so deep it reaches to the depths of discouragement, despair, depression, doubt and fear. When you feel shut down, isolated, nothing left, Jesus is with you, and you can never be lost to God's love. We all face hardships. They come in many forms. I had to overcome sexual abuse, divorces, domestic violence and verbal abuse. These could have caused me to live in fear that I have been abandoned by God. But it is impossible to be separated from God. His death is proof of his unconquerable love. Nothing can stop Christ's constant presence and light in us. No matter what happens to us, no matter where we are, we can never be separated.

"For I am convinced that neither death nor life, neither angels nor demons, neither the present nor the future, nor any powers, neither height nor depth, nor anything else in all creation, will be able to separate us from the love of God that is in Christ Jesus our Lord." (Romans 8:38-39)

People asked me what changed. I never really had an answer until I wrote it down that day after I was in a major season of re-evaluation and a calling over my life that day in the shower. I stopped focusing so much on *who* I was and *who* I wanted to be and stepped into the purpose and fullness of *who* I belonged to and *who* I was called to be.

Never doubt Gods ability and power to work in you and through you. There is purpose beyond your pain. God will exceed your expectations. Not by a little blessing, or a little increase. God is going to exceed it abundantly and more than you could ever dream.

CHAPTER 1

Stronger than the Setback

THE DOOR WAS LOCKED. THE BATHROOM WAS ALL steamed up. I was playing worship songs turned up on my phone to muffle the tears and crying that I could not control as I wept on the floor of my tiny little shower. I was broken. Overcome by the reality that surrounded me. All the pain of years of abuse just wearing on me, like a tire on a car, all the miles that have worn down the tread. Except I was the tire, needing repair. I had lost my tread. I was sick and tired of living in this painful season. Years of painful experiences, built up layers upon layers, like a Florida car under a Spring Oak tree. Lots of layers of pollen. What my spirit needed was a good tire change and a car wash. I got the car wash part done.

Now the real work needed to start. I was in a major season of evaluation. So I started peeling the layers back one by one. As a child I was physically abused. Physically and mentally abused. I never truly got help for it until later in my young adulthood, but we will talk about that in a later chapter. Because of the abuse I suffered it bled over to my teen years. As a teenager I started looking for attention, seeking love from men. Being promiscuous to get attention in a non-healthy way. The only attention I ever got was from boys. I was invited by a local friend to youth group at a church she attended. I never knew what young life was until then. It was the first time I felt accepted. I did not have to try to be something I was not. Although I still felt alone. I wasn't like the other girls. Raised from a happy healthy family, sitting around their dinner table together. Talking about God, being prayed over.

I never sat at a dinner table growing up. We ate dinner in front of a TV, or I would take it to my room alone. We had a home cooked meal about once a week. She technically was my step-mother as my biological mother left my brother and I when we were little with my Father, but she was Mom to me. So it started as a little girl, abandoned and alone. I had a troubled brother, who I learned in my adulthood did some pretty disturbing things. My mother who raised me had to keep a very close eye on me to make sure my brother didn't cause harm to me, at least that's what I discovered reading recently in old Court papers from when we were younger. Most of my younger childhood years were good. We went on normal family vacations. Theme parks, beach, out to Denny's, which was our favorite. We would be so excited when we would order our very own orange juice.

My parents were hard workers for the most part, my mother putting herself through nursing school at thirty six years old to provide for our family. My Father, a convicted felon, a motorcy-cle mechanic, never really held a solid job. He was around but never involved. He met my biological mother at a gentlemen's entertainment club where she worked full-time. Most of what I remember as a small child was spending a lot of time at my grand-mother's house in Hialeah; he stayed out in the garage most of my childhood and into the adult years. Most for my life I thought he truly was never comfortable in his own skin unless he was work-ing on motorcycles. My mother and father could not stand each other. There was a lot of *felt underlying chaos* in my household. My parents did their best but their marriage was a disaster. Our family foundation was built on yelling, fighting, throwing plates, it really was a parenting goal of mine NOT! My mother had a temper and my father was really good at pushing it. My Dad was broken and not able to be there for us. He was battling some really dark stuff, drugs and years of alcohol abuse, and financial crimes.

I felt very alone as a little girl, in a large family, full of unex-pressed, pent up deep emotions. I naturally leaned toward being the talkative, controller, performer to try and make everyone get along; I was not brought up in church. The best years of my childhood were playing with my sisters. We used to jump the alley behind our house and play while my mother would study. We grew up in Miami and moved to St. Augustine when I was about nine or ten years old. Funny thing was my great great grandparents were born and raised in St. Augustine. So tech-nically I moved back home. They were original Minorcans. My great great grandmother traveled from Ireland to Ellis Island, New York when she was fifteen years old and settled in St. Augustine, which I did not find out until my adult life.

Fast forward to my teenage years, broken, lost not knowing my real family and abandoned I was at a young life church camp in Hilton Head, SC with a brand new Bible in my hand. The youth Pastor wrote my name in it. I remember the gold pages, the line that said "Occasion." What was the occasion; she laughed and said, "You have accepted Jesus as your Lord and Savior." It was a church camp summer vacation I will never forgot. It answered so many questions for me. I vividly recall asking what the lines in red meant. If that gives you an idea of how much I really didn't know. I was crying on my knees during worship, sitting cross legged on a conference room floor. Asking God, "Am I not worthy?" I was fifteen years old, sexually abused by a then boyfriend early that winter. He told me it was my fault. I skipped school that afternoon.

I felt like it was my fault. I had put myself into a really dangerous situation. I remember telling my mom months later, and she slapped me in the face. She called me a very ugly derogatory name, and how could I have been so stupid. After that, I never spoke of it again until now. I told my older sister to try and be cool. After that I stopped caring. I made just enough to pass school. I made a passing GPA to play sports that was the only thing I ever felt good at, that and making people laugh. I absorbed my mother's emotional issues to try to off burden her load. My mother would share with my sisters and me very intimate details of her pain and struggle even issues with her and my father, when I was too young to understand, carry or support her in any way. I often carried burdens in my heart for my mother and my parents that I was spiritually and emotionally unable to carry at my age. The burden was an overwhelming feeling what I felt, hearing what I heard, and seeing what I saw. It was mixed with a genuine need for my Dad to scoop me up in his arms but he was emotionally disconnected and therefore, unable to hold me and tell me it was going to be okay, because was it actually going to be okay? I don't think anyone in my family really knew.

I remember in 8th grade I made a D on my interim report and my mother grabbed my cheerleader uniform, shoes, bows all the bells and whistles, threw it in the burn barrel and made me watch it burn. My father just stood there smoking his cigarette and drinking his beer and did not say one word. I wanted him to say something, anything. But not one word. My mother told me I was a looser and a failure. How come I couldn't be more like my sister, the smart one? A part of me grew cold that day. It didn't matter what I did. I was always getting in trouble. No matter how hard I tried to please her, no matter how hard I tried to earn her love. I was never good enough. I was sitting on the floor of that stale conference room, with all the chairs pushed to the side of the wall, sitting next to a bunch of teenager kids from all around crying. Burying all the secrets I have been carrying. I went for a walk that night on the beach and sat there. I told God everything that I sinned for. I gave it all to him. I didn't want to go home. I found hope at that church camp. I knew something greater, bigger than I could ever imagined loved me. That was the first time I felt loved. Surrounded by strangers, even my friend who invited me I don't think knew what I had been through. The only other person I ever told was a church camp Pastor who was someone's parent. I cried in the hallway to her after that walk on that beach alone and poured my heart onto her. She had no idea. She left and came back with a folded up piece of paper tucked in my Bible. She told me to start there. To read those scriptures and prayed over me. It was the first time I felt free. But that wasn't it. I wish I could say that I left that camp and it was all blessings from there, but it wasn't. I came home, and my mother told me I had been brain-washed. She took both me and my sister's Bible and threw them in the trash. I remember running to the trash can, digging it out and told her she was going to burn in Hell for that. I ran to my room and hid my Bible. I didn't care what she said to me but that was the only thing that made me feel whole – the Bible. She slapped me and told me if she found it, she was going to throw it away. She never did find it. I tucked it away and wrapped it up in an old tee-shirt. I had to clean the spaghetti sauce off one side, but I didn't care; it was perfect and I still had that piece of paper tucked in Romans 8.

"Therefore, there is no condemnation for those who are in Christ Jesus because through Christ Jesus the law of the spirit who gives life has set you free from the law of sin and death. For what the law was powerless to do because it was weakened by the flesh, God did by sending his own Son in the likeness of sinful flesh to be a sin offering. And so he condemned sin in the flesh. In order that the righteous requirement of the law might be fully met in us, who do not live according to the flesh but according to the Spirit."

That piece of paper folded up said, "There are two choices, those who are dominated by their sinful nature, and those who are controlled by the Holy Spirit. All of us would be in the first category, if Jesus hadn't offered us a way out. Once you said yes to Jesus, you started following him and that brings life and peace. Center your life on God. She circled that. WWJD. Yup, I am a millennial and we use to write that on everything.

After that summer, it was the same if not worse. I went to young life on Wednesdays light but couldn't escape. I was abandoned, alone, "Burnt Goods" I used to say heavily to myself. So what was the point? I was on a nowhere track, with a God I was angry at for abandoning me. I became more promiscuous, sneaking out at night, ran away to a friend's house, begged her father to let me live with them. The police showed up and said, "We can take you home, or you can go to the Youth Crisis Center." I chose YCC. It was the first time I ever spoke to a Counselor. It was the first time I went to sleep that night without being yelled at. I woke up the next day, had a bowl of cereal at a table with a social worker and she asked if I wanted something to read. I asked if she had a Bible. She smiled, and handed me one. It was so weird to me that I could openly read the Bible and not have to hide it; I wasn't in trouble for it.

Little did I know, my mother showed up, dressed up very beautifully with her pearls and stockings. The three of us sitting in the Counselor's office, and that Bible in my hand. I stopped listening and blacked out after what felt like a few minutes. She said I hated her, and was rebelling. That I was sneaking out and having sexual intercourse with a ton of guys. It was so far from the truth. I cried and tried to get up but they wouldn't allow me to leave. I knew, nobody was going to listen to me. So I shut down. Did what they asked me, wrote her an apology letter, and didn't say a word on the drive home. I was so angry. I was angry at God; I hated her but most importantly I hated myself. I was making poor choices. I hated myself so much; I would do things to hate myself more. It was a toxic pattern. I ended up pregnant at seventeen, my junior summer. I told my mother, and she told me to have an abortion or move out. I started packing that night and moved out the next morning. Thankfully, his family were believers. They were the nicest people. I really think of it as I had no business getting pregnant, no business getting married at age eighteen. I graduated high school, and was a mother at eighteen. His parents taught me how to cook. They taught me a lot of firsts as a woman. My Mother and I reconciled before my son was born. My Dad had called and said, "Your Mother said she's sorry, and wants you to come home, your husband and you can live in the back house." We had a second home on the property. I told him she had to personally call me and apologize for all of it, or I was not going home. I saw moving home as an opportunity for a young new family, to live in our own home and raise a family. It worked well for a little while; unfortunately, my issues would rear its ugly head once again. We ended up separating when my son was two. The only way I knew how to love someone was to leave.

Pain was what I knew, that was the love I was used to. A broken childhood, a broken adolescence, and a divorced single mom. Fast forward I then got into another relationship, fueled by alcohol, domestic violence and another pregnancy. I was really doing a great job of screwing up my life. I royally had just gone from one bad relationship to another. I had no business once again getting into a relationship so broken, so vulnerable, and in so much pain. I did a great job of putting on a façade. Going to college full-time in nursing school, working two jobs, moving back home to my mother's house to help her pay for her bills. My Father and my Mother ended up divorcing when I was twenty three. My Father had put our home into foreclosure for the third time. I recently had been in an auto accident and took the insurance check for my vehicle and went to the local bank and paid three months of their mortgage. Did I want to? Heck no. Did I also have three younger siblings living there? Yes. So I did. Never to see a penny again from that. I never regretted that. My Mother had worked so hard, being twenty three at the time it felt like it kind of clicked for me. My Father ruined her. Financially, emotionally and spiritually. She never signed up for that. She raised her siblings at a young age, and now raising her children by herself. My Dad did a really good job of blowing money and doing drugs. He wasn't as good at hiding it as he thought he was. He owed people tons of money. Wrote very large bad checks and went to jail for almost a year. I was the middle child and their problems got taken out on me. A deep sadness engulfed me. I was supposed to be happy for my Mom that she was set free, but I wasn't. I was angry that I was a child picking up the pieces for my parents. No one helped me. No one helped me pick up the pieces. I was pissed, can I say pissed? Yes, I looked up the definition – *Very annoyed; angry.*

Guess what comes next? Those ugly issues rearing its head again. There I was, in the next toxic relationship, ended up pregnant. Domestic violence, break up, get back together, break up, married and divorced. You're probably asking yourself, "Gosh! When is this girl going to learn?" I asked myself that a lot. I didn't. I was arrested a few times. A criminal. I didn't care anymore. I really didn't. Like God, yay, I'm no good at this; I am just like my Father. The Mother I did love, I never felt like she did love me. I was living a reckless life and lost my purpose. If I had a calling on my life, God probably rescinded that. I was out of control. I was desperate and screaming for attention. I had a heavy heart, heaviness of failure over my life, from my family, my friends, and my peers. I was in trouble.

My thoughts and emotional pain were beyond repair, at least that's what I felt. Imagine, being spit at in the face, having a drink thrown on you, and being told you're worthless. Being choked because you dumped a bottle of liquor down the drain, because you got tired of cleaning up the vomit and staying awake all night to make sure your spouse doesn't aspirate in his own vomit.

Yay, it was a glamorous life. I highly don't recommend it. That whole stay in school, and stay out of trouble, actually means something. So the shower story picks up right here. Still haven't changed that "Spiritual tire." I put a spare on multiple times, just doing a quick fix, but never replaced it. I was not a good mechanic. I was angry at God. Like God, please, I am so trapped. Trapped from my past, thoughts, emotions, pain, insecurities, self-esteem all the big hitters. I was trapped in a cycle of living that had me questioning my sanity. Needless to say, I was in turmoil, and something had to give.

I wanted to change, but I felt like I was too far gone. Something deep-rooted in me was tugging at my heart – Jesus. "Hello, you-hoo, you done screwing up your life? I'm here waiting, just let me know when you're ready, you can't be a victim forever." I made a choice. Completely surrender my mind, will, heart, and emotions back over to God, or there is a chance I will continue on this reckless road, never see my children again, and succumb to the darkness I felt trying to crawl back in my life. When God spoke to me in the shower that day, it was a pivotal shift in my life. There was no denying it, no shaking that feeling. It was the first time in fifteen years I felt God holding me. Cradling the crying little girl. God unlocked the prison cell I had kept my mind and body in. Because of that day, I never stopped reading, pressing, learning, spiritually learning everything about God. I was able to meet a Christian man who loves me and all of my past. He got the wife who now writes scriptures on the bathroom mirrors with lipstick, blares worship music, is still Sassy but Saved, the two step-children, the two animals. We now have a daughter. If you would have asked me whether I would eventually marry the man of my dreams, I would have laughed at you.

But you know what, I finally changed that tire. I went to the "Spiritual mechanic shop." It needed a full work up, "Spiritual inventory." God had stripped all those layers off. He washed me clean of my sin, pure as white. God took all those broken things and made them so beautiful. I am here to tell you if you can believe anyone, believe me. God loves you, all of you. He doesn't call the qualified, he qualifies the called. I am as unqualified as they come. I have no theology background, no formal pastoral experience. I don't have anything to give you except offer you salvation and help you find your purpose beyond your pain.

God had come flooding back into my life like that teenage girl sitting on a conference room floor, crying, smiling, and knowing her worth all over again. He wrapped His arms around me that day. The Holy Spirit comforting me in all-surrounding embrace. It was overwhelming and I was vulnerable, yet at the same time peaceful. I had let God into the most barricaded, most defense heavy sacred, and scariest parts of my heart. He replaced all my fears with confidence with security. I had a purpose. I was a Mother to my beautiful children.

> "I am the way and the truth and the life. No one comes
> to the Father except through me. If you really know
> me, you will know my Father as well."

> (John 14:6-7)

God is the reality of all His promises. That is the truth I choose to believe. Thank you, God, for providing a sure way to get to you.

God chose to join his divine life to ours, both now and eternally. Jesus is, in truth, the only living way to the Father. Give it to God, do not let your hearts be troubled with the pain, do not be afraid. It amazing how He can replace all your fears and doubts. What I mean by that is all those years I was a prisoner to my life, I had the answer all along. I had the solution. When we declare Jesus as our Lord and Savior and make a public declaration and receive His truth, we are instantaneously given the gift of the Holy Spirit to share with and receive truth from.

> That means with that base every person can find purpose beyond their pain no matter your past, pain, how you feel or what you have been through.

> (1 John 4:13-18) (Romans 5:5, 8:9) (2 Corinthians 1:22) (Romans 8:16)

Family is your first fellowship. That will be your greatest ministry. Our family was doing our daily Bible study, and my children asked me how old I was when I went to my first church camp. I paused for a good few minutes. I went to the bookshelf, I took down that very first Bible given to me at church camp and showed the kids. My oldest, who is a teenager, also goes to church camp every summer. He is fifteen. I cried and gave him a hug. He did not understand what happened in that moment. I hugged him tightly and told him not to worry about it. He was nothing like me. He was the fifteen year old I wanted to be. I love all my children deeply but that night I gave him multiple hugs, prayed over him, and made sure he knew how proud I am of him and how smart he is. What he had that I never had at his age was sanctified time of fellowship for God and family. Thank you, God, for what *you do* through me and in me to be able to sanctify time in our family *for you.*

CHAPTER 2

Who's in Charge?

WELL, IT CERTAINLY WAS NOT ME ANYMORE. I received Christ as a teenager at the age of fifteen but did not live as a free child of God until I truly gave it all to Him. Every day since that moment God came to deliver me in the shower, I was never the same anymore. That was a very pivotal point for me. I had to make a choice. But I was so frozen, imprisoned in my shame and guilt and everyone that ever hurt me, I did not feel equipped nor did I even feel that I deserved the right to even have that choice. I was buried in the trenches of remorse and depression. I knew deep down in my heart that I was a woman of God, a Mother to my two beautiful boys. It was enough. Enough of being a victim, dragged by the enemy, sinking his claws, and his dark shadow trying to absorb me. I felt like in that moment, I was looking down at my life. I was experiencing an outer look in. Like girl, you have got to fix your life right now! I was never going to fulfill my calling unless I got out of the comfort zone of sleeping with the pain. Have you heard the saying, "If it was easy, everyone would do it?"

My Mother used to say that all the time, now I can say I fully understand what that means. Doing the right thing isn't always easy, spiritual growth takes discipline. Getting out of your comfort zone, and following your calling is spiritual freedom. You are not trapped on the "now" or the "when I accomplish this or I can follow my calling if only I had the right circumstance or degree." Circumstances don't determine my choice. I don't need certain circumstances to follow Gods calling on my life. I really had to do a self-inventory, that no matter how much I made a mess of my life, experiencing physical, sexual, mental trauma I couldn't allow those circumstances to stunt my spiritual freedom or I could choose to focus on becoming the best version of yourself. Focus on who you're called to be, and focus on what you do. You can't focus on what happened in the past and other people. You can't stay in the left lane of pain. It's draining you; you're not that kind of person, mom, wife, preacher, pastor, blogger, author that's not you. Focus on the biblical picture of your life. With God, spirit at the center. *Pneuma* is an Ancient Greek word for 'breathe, spirit, soul.' Spirit of life. The Holy Spirit is living in you. Your spirit determines your identity. Your spirit made to fully contain God, speaks to God (spirit to spirit) when we want to know what God is thinking, the Holy Spirit talks to us. Because the spirit of God is in us. Our soul consists of our mind, consists of our will, our decisions and determinations. Your emotions, what you're feeling, encompasses your personality. The *renewal* comes in the mind, will and emotions. Everything our soul wants to do, our body encompasses. That is the biblical picture of you. That's where becoming the *best* version of you happens right here. Of our best version of us comes from our character. That's our actions and how we treat people. Your attitude, your thoughts, your core values and your beliefs systems and what you think about life. Your attitude is grounded on your belief system. Your attitude about what you think about life goes deep into your belief system. You have to dig deep spiritually if you don't like where your attitude is. Because if you have a bad attitude about life, you're not putting your faith on the front line. No matter what circumstance you're in, if you have the spirit of, "I know God has a calling on my life, over me, over my family. I am going to choose to trust in God and not myself and my feelings." Feelings are your emotions that you feel. Emotions have no moral value. See, emotions are like waves, you get to choose which one you ride. You could be angry about the situation, and not sin. Emotions tell you what's going on, our choices are one hundred percent our responsibility. You get to choose – What your attitude is about life? How you feel about life? And the choices in your life.

Ask yourself this, "What do I need to Steward in my life? Is this in my control? Whatever struggle, difficulty, whatever season that looks like for you, you get to choose is this in my control?" We have full responsibility over our choices. That is where our personal choices are. People who follow their calling use choice to define them not circumstances. This is the most spiritual invest- ment you can do for yourself; fulfill your calling, *trusting in God!* I hope these tips help you to utilize in your life, to enjoy your life, find balance in it, because God is really in charge and the quicker we agree in that you will find your life in balance, spiritually, emotionally and physically.

It was such a hard season for me, I naturally like to be in control, or at least think I am in control of my life. The most gut wrenching question I asked myself was this, and if you're like me ask yourself this question.

God reveal to me where did control become my weapon of choice to protect myself?

If that's you, I want you to write it down. Write it in this book or wherever you want. I had to give it up. I would walk around, helping the children with their homework, cooking dinner, gardening, when I used to run, but seriously I used to be quite the athlete, I would say to myself over and over, "Surrender the control to Jesus, it's not yours." I wrote it on my bathroom mirror. But if you're like me, man I wish I could tell you girl, you will say to yourself once you give up that battle, "Wow I feel so much better." I would beg and cry out, "Holy Spirit, what do you have for me to pick up instead?" God had so much in store for me, but I had to give that up first. So ask yourself, "What does Jesus, the way maker, perfect all-knowing God, what does He have for you instead?" Forgive yourself girl. You are kind, smart, and beautiful. My prayer for you is to remain in His Love. (John 15:1-7). Don't stress over it, now that you realize you are not in control. You have given it to God now; now what? Nothing, that's the beauty of it. It is His, it is all His. Jesus commands us not to worry. But how can we avoid it? Only our faith can free us from the anxiety caused by us trying to control our lives and the things in it. Working and planning responsibility are good; schedules are great and keep this wife and momma sane, believe me. But dwelling on all of ways our planning could go wrong is bad. Worry is pointless because it can't fill any of our needs; worry is foolish because the Creator of the universe loves us and knows what we need. He promises to meet all our real needs, but not necessarily all our desires.

Then Jesus said to his disciples:

"Therefore I tell you, do not worry about your life, what you will eat; or about your body, what you will wear. For life is more than food, and the body more than clothes. Consider the ravens: They do not sow or reap, they have no store room or barn; yet God feeds them. And how much more valuable you are than birds! Who of you by worrying can add a single hour to your life? Since you cannot do this very little thing, why do you worry about the rest?"

(Luke 12: 22-26)

I knew that God could set me free from my insecurities and painful past but I had lived all of my life comfortable in my chains. I understood that He wanted to deal with the chains in my life, so I asked Him to take my shaking hand and walk me to the other side, to freedom. And He did. It's a cliché I know, but it's true. I felt like a completely different person. I see things so differently now. The world of truth outside the walls of that prison of lies is so freeing. There is purpose beyond the pain. Seeking the Kingdom of God above all else means making Jesus the Lord and King of your life. He must control every area – your work, play, plans, and relationships. *Is the Kingdom only one of your many concerns, or is it central to all you do? Are you holding back any areas of your life from God's control?* As Lord and Creator, He wants to help provide what you need as well as guide how you use what he provides.

Spiritually growing takes discipline

Be called, step out of your comfort zone.

If you can take one thing and walk away with today, it is that if you make daily choices and focus on God you will learn powerful things for your tool belt to apply to your life and live with purpose, passion, and walk in boldness. To live a life of leadership and inspiration and influencer as a woman.

CHAPTER 3

Failing Flawlessly

WE NEED MORE THAN A LEADER ON OUR ROAD TO freedom, just handing over the control back to God. Yah, it doesn't stop there. We need someone to stick around and empower us to remain free. We need a Savior – one who keeps on saving. Many people only think of salvation as their initial invitation for Christ to forgive them and come into their lives. Look, although we need to be *saved* from eternal separation from God only once, Christ continues His saving work in us for the rest of our lives.

Can you think of a few potential disasters from which Christ saved you since your initial experience of salvation?

I have had many, and thank God for dodging those disasters. By now reading this, you know I definitely wasn't good at that. I had to learn how to love myself again. How to be kind again. I had to keep going back to the word, to Jesus. I thought, "Well, hey God; I am like saved now, so we're square, right?" I turned my life around. Look at me I'm doing so great, no longer bound by the chains, but no, unfortunately there was a good dose of self-aware-ness I had for my choices. I had failed flawlessly. Free from the imperfections of judgement, defected opinions; I did not care anymore. I perfectly failed but realized we all do. What a dramatic shift in emotion and way of thinking. God came to rule the heaven and earth. I stopped beating myself up. The enemy has already been defeated. Why was I still feeling guilty and ashamed? We as women, put an immense amount of pressure on ourselves. What about cultivating a culture of compassion over competition? It's not about who has the bigger house, the greener lawn, the Ph.D., or is in a supportive role at minimum wage. We do not all have to knock each other down, running into black Friday to grab the best gifts while putting on our social media hashtag 'thankful', while leaving our family for greed. I dream for a day to see all women finding spiritual freedom and restored in the perfect Love Jesus has for them. *Does your life align with Gods calling on your life?* If it does not, then what your putting your energy into, and absorbing your time is stealing the joy from your life. God has a calling on your life and a fulfilling love that is endless.

Do you find comfort in Jesus or is it something else stealing your joy?

> "The Lord is the Spirit, and where the Spirit of the
> Lord is, there is freedom."

> (2 Corinthians 3:17)

Your wounds, your trauma, your chains, whatever that looks like for you, the wounds you have carried that are yours not to carry, God wants to take your wounds and turn them into a well, a beautiful well that can feed everyone around you. God wants to use your wounds to heal others. He is the ultimate healer. The very ones who wounded you, you can forgive them. Your wounds are a part of the mission. Some of you are running away from them, living in denial, we are now free from those wounds, and your wounds when healed, you have the capacity and knowledge to help stand in the gap for others and gently help them through that season of finding freedom. Loving one another, filled with a heart to *serve* for Him, *through* Him. Look at those wounds, healed, closed, pure made beautifully broken and united in Gods Kingdom; you are an extension of the Ultimate healer's hand. It's not about more self-love for yourself, it's about more love for one another. Less judging of one another, less gossiping, but more *loving*.

"Comfort, comfort my people, says your God." (Isaiah 40:1)

Oh, how I thank God for tender words He has spoken to me after I failed flawlessly. We stand to receive much healing from God's words of comfort. Sometimes I wonder why He continues to be so faithful. Yes, He is faithful to rebuke or how would we otherwise learn from our rebellion? But He is also compassionate in His comfort. **God hears the cry of the oppressed**. God even hears the cries of those who have oppressed as a result of sin and rebellion. We must never stop believing God cares about those in physical, emotional, mental, or spiritual prisons. Everything that concerns us is in God's domain. God issued Isaiah 61:1-4 as a response to the captivity He foresaw as He looked down on rebellious Judah. Isaiah, the Prophet was the son of Amoz. He was calling the nation of Judah back to God and to tell of Gods salvation through the Messiah. Think of Isaiah as like Gods spokesperson. He was the messenger to Judah.

Like Israel and Judah, much of our own captivity by pain is caused by failure to remove obstacles of unbelief, pride, idolatry, prayerlessness and spirit-quenching legalism; yet God still saves us to a spacious redeemed place free from our pain and abuse we once suffered.

I am so thankful God can take historic, fallen, broken insecurities, relationships, and families and turn them into the Bride of Jesus. It's a covenant commitment to forgive. Forgiveness is tied to the mission. You get to stand on behalf of other people, and forgive them. The people who offended you, you can look them in the eye and say, "You are forgiven."

———————

1. I want you to write all the failures you feel you have had in your life. It can be on a piece of paper, fast food napkin in your glove department, or a beautiful piece of stationary.

2. Write down and identify obvious patterns or circumstances that have become rocks of shame to your past.

Take it easy and gentle on yourself. Work through these one at a time as you channel the Holy Spirit to guide you.

3. Now, number them. I want you to find the truth in the word God has over your life for each one of those failures you believed over your life. Don't rush it, set aside time to dig into the Bible.

4. After you have written down the truths and scriptures over your life, put them away, safety tucked away but where you can still see them every day. Pray over them. Speak the scriptures over your life. Memorize your favorite ones. You may feel nothing at first, that's alright; finding freedom beyond your pain changes and takes time. You can read them daily or three times a day, whatever works for you.

5. As you walk these out with Jesus, and encounter the healer, and lover of your soul, ask what shame you've been holding on to as a part of your identity. As a visual illustration, take that shame, ball it up in your hands and give it to Jesus. Imagine the love in His eyes, with a smile on his face, as He reaches out and takes it out of your hands. Now, what can you do in return for Jesus?

Speak this prayer over you:

"Jesus, I love you, I am no longer going to define my failures to your worth. My worth is in you. You chose me as your very own, lord give me patience, calmness, and confidence that God you are in control of my life, and over my life. I release the shame and guilt. The enemy has no authority over my heart, home and mind. I have nothing to hide anymore. I am no longer buried in the shadows of those who hurt me. God, you take me as I am. Your love reminds me that my true identity is in you. I will no longer walk in shame of my past but in the truth and love that has set me free." Amen.

CHAPTER 4

Divorce and Decaf

"So if the son sets you free, you will be free indeed."

(John 8:36)

I WANT TO TELL YOU A STORY. IT'S THE STORY OF Jonah and the Whale. I find that many adults know about the story, but many know only that Jonah got swallowed by a whale/big fish. What they don't know is the reason or the moral to this timeless scripture. I would like to retell it to you in a modern telling. Jonah was the son of Mr. & Mrs. Amittai. His name means "dove." We know nothing about his lineage — he was not related to any king or prophets. He was just a regular Joe. (Bad pun intended.) At some indeterminate age, Jonah gets a call from God. God says, "Jonah, there's something I want you to do in a city to the east." Jonah gets on a boat going west. Jonah goes below deck and goes to sleep. Jonah awakes in the middle of a huge storm that threatens the ship. Jonah knows that he has endangered the lives of the other passengers, so he jumps into the water, calming the sea.

The big fish swallows him whole. Jonah spends days in the fish contemplating his life. It is there, in the dark depths, that he says one of the most beautiful prayers in the Bible. After he has lost all hope, he says, "I was deader than dead until I remembered you, God." Man can we just pause right there, that's deep. I don't know if you have ever been there, but I have, and that reignited to my bones. Jonah in that moment acknowledges his choices. Jonah should have laid off the caffeine … kidding. But seriously God gave him specific instructions and he went his way. I totally can relate. Back to the story, God talks to the fish and the fish delivers Jonah to Nineveh—a city as populated as New Delhi. Nineveh is where Jonah was told to go in the first place. Jonah walks for three days to the center of town and declares, "Hey, listen up! You all are not living the way you are supposed to be living—if only according to your own conscience." The inhabitants of Nineveh declare a fast—they mourn their loss of idealism as though it were a lost loved one.

They grieve for their own mortality. They weep for all not living the simple, joyful lives they knew they should be living. They cry for reasons hidden but present deep in their hearts. Then The King of Nineveh, when he hears of what his people are doing, joins in their fast and their mourning. And—in what must have been perceived as a bit of biblical humor—the people of Nineveh even dress their cattle in mourning clothes. This prayer Jonah offers is not about asking for anything. It is an honest outpouring of the heart. And, here is a great quote about prayer by David Mamet:

"The purpose of prayer is not to be about an interces-
sion in the material world, but to lay down, for the
time of prayer, one's confusion and rage and sorrow
at one's powerlessness."

Point is what Jonah was called to do—as difficult as it
might have seemed to him in the first place—wound
up not being that difficult to do once he actually did
it! (Jonah 1:1-3)

There is a litany of things that we know we "should be doing"
and that we choose to avoid. We know that some of the things on
the "to do" list just get heavier the longer we avoid them. We know
that the only person we are really inconveniencing by avoiding
them is us. I call this 'Divorce and Decaf.' I went through some
pretty bad relationships. I had some really ugly divorces. Yes, it
is plural. I have been divorced twice. I chose to follow my path
and not Gods. It was devastating to my children. I caused them
the pain that I wish they never had to feel. Years of trying to fix
my children's insecurity as they went through some pretty rough
times, and I will never be able to take that back. I was judged by
my friends, peers and society because I was divorced. I want you
to walk with me right here, I was in a season of getting out of a
really bad relationship and someone had the audacity to say to
me, "Is anyone going to want to be with a woman who has two
children with two different Fathers?" If I don't tell you the Gods
to honest truth, I had to take the Miami out of me like, "Girl, you
don't know me but I am fresh off the road of getting my life back

on track, and let me tell you I am Holy enough to pray for you and Hood enough to swing on you." Just kidding, well in my head I wasn't, but I was thinking that The Holy Spirit needs to come up here and snatch me in check.

It was a moment I had to really pause, and get a grip on my emotions; I mean that remark offended every bone, blood vessel, cell in my body. But you know what God said to me, not poor you, not poor Aimee, he said, "Aimee those are her issues and not yours. You can choose to be upset with that and make that your issue, or you can put your faith in me regardless of whether you have failed in your life." This scripture I had to memorize for a few days and speak this over my life. Once again, I felt those old doubts, emotions, fear trying to sneak back into my life.

"Do not let your faith fail you even though you failed."

(Luke 22:33-34)

I had every right to be angry, being angry is not a sin, but how you react, you are in control of. I can sit here and be angry at everyone who ever hurt me, I could be a victim, and I could somber in self-pity and sit on the couch in isolation. But can I tell you something, I have been that girl before. I have been so depressed that even the idea of getting in the shower and washing my hair was miserable. I would have to mentally and physically psych myself up to get moving. In that scripture I mentioned above in Luke, it is so much more important to not let my emotions and reactions be dulled by someone else's issues, don't let your mind and spirit be dulled but those kind of things or those kind of people, because the real focus and fight is not being anxious about all those fears and insecurities the enemy is trying to speak over you and your life. I had to refocus my life and start getting spiritually fit because the real fight is getting spiritually aligned and staying spiritually aligned so that I will be ready to move at Gods command. **This means working faithfully at the tasks God has given us. Not what the enemy says over us.**

I called that time in my life Decaf. No control, no caffeine, no stimulants. I was feeding myself so many things that caused the anxiety, the doubt. I took back my life, got rid of the depression, gave my life back to God, received Gods love but I was still feeding my spirit with things that were crippling my emotions. Jesus commands us not to worry. But how can we avoid it? Only faith can free us from the anxiety caused covetousness. I cut out caffeine and went to decaf for a while. I had to decaffeinate all those toxic people and relationships in my life. Here are some questions you can write out if you want to decaffeinate those people and relationships in your life. This is necessary if you want to walk in the path of spiritual freedom.

———————

1. Write down the name(s) that have said something hurtful to you or have caused you emotional, physical or mental pain?

2. I want you to write how it made you feel when they hurt you.

3. Now visualize what you wrote, you are staring them in the face. Now have the heart of bravery to stare your pain in the face. Hold hands with the Healer and ball that pain up into a perfectly shaped ball.

4. Hand over that tightly shaped ball of pain over the Healer. He is still holding your other hand.

   Pray this out loud over that ball you handed over to Jesus.

   (Psalm 55:22-23)

"Cast your cares on the Lord, and he will sustain you; he will never let the righteous be shaken. But you, God will bring down the wicked into the pit of decay, the bloodthirsty and deceitful will not live out half their days. But as for me, I trust you." My beautiful friend, take a deep breath. You have let that part of you go. You feel a weight has been lifted off your chest. If you need to pause and pick this up later, go ahead. You do not need permission. Marinate in this moment. That bounty is no longer over you. Speak it, shout it, declare it, you are fearlessly and wonderfully made. You have decaffeinated that season out! When all seems dark, one truth still shines bright: When God is for us, those against us will never succeed. You are loved, you are safe, and you are protected by the almighty Father. I want to close out in this beautiful prayer a friend sent to me when I was walking away from a divorce and decaffeinating my life.

> "You, God, are a shield around me. You protect me from the enemy who seeks to destroy, and you will not let me be put to shame. Your arm is mighty, and your word is powerful."
>
> (Psalm 3:3, 12:7, 25:20, Exodus 15:9, Luke 1:51, Hebrews 1:3)

> When the enemy attacks her, let her faith in you protect her so that she may stand her ground. Bring your word to her mind so that she may turn aside his assaults and fight the good fight. Help her to remember that you give us the victory through Christ.
>
> (Ephesians 6:10-18, 1 Timothy 6:12, 1 Corinthians 15:57)

You have conquered and disarmed the spiritual powers, and everything is in complete submission to you. Because of the cross (say your name) is a new creation, and nothing can separate her from your amazing, unfailing love. The enemy is defeated. You have crushed his head.

(Genesis 3:15) Amen.

CHAPTER 5

External Restorations

"And when they climbed into the boat, the wind died down.
Then those who were in the boat worshiped him, saying,
'Truly you are the son of God.'"

(Matthew 13:32-33)

ALTHOUGH WE START OUT WITH GOOD INTENTIONS, sometimes our faith falters. This doesn't necessarily mean we have failed. When Peter's faith faltered, he was afraid, but he still looked to Christ. When you are apprehensive about the troubles or fear of not knowing what your future looks like and doubt Christ's presence or ability to help, you must remember that He is the *only* one who can really help. This was a season I learned to wait. Lewis Smedes once said, "Waiting is the hardest work of hope." Easier to type and quote than it is to walk it out. Let me tell you, I do not like surprises. I do not like not knowing plans. What we're going to do? I have had my husband kindly say that I have control issues. I am a major type A personality. Waiting patiently is not a strong suit for me. I would fairly say society is not full of patient people. We tend to be horn-beep beep move, microwaving, fed-ex mailing, fast-food eating, in a self-checkout kind of hurry. We don't like to wait in traffic, hold on the phone, wait in lines in the store, or wait for our amazon packages to arrive. Like Amazon Prime, I have to wait two days, thinking to myself, "That's terrible; I thought that's why I have Prime." We have all been guilty of it at one time in our lives or another.

So how good are you at waiting? Are you good at remodels, external restorations? I for one struggle with remodels because I do not enjoy the process. It's not instantly fixed or re-painted, I was the kind of girl who wanted it complete in one day. One whole day, that's it. If I couldn't have that, I did not want it. Most of us don't like waiting very much, so we like the fact that Matthew shows Jesus to be the Lord of urgent action. Three times in just a few sentences Matthew uses the word *immediately* – always of Jesus: Jesus made the disciples get into a boat and go on ahead of him "*immediately*." When the disciples thought they were seeing a ghost and cried out in fear, Jesus answered them "*immediately*." When Peter began to sink and cried out for help, Jesus "*immediately*" reached out his hand and caught him. Jesus' actions are swift, discerning, and decisive. He doesn't waste a beep beep-drive through, or a hold on the phone; amazon prime took two days and delivered to the wrong door. Ya'll feel me yet?

What I am trying to illustrate from this story is that if we can learn one thing from Peter, Paul, and Matthew is that we are not forsaken, that the Lord watches over us unseen … that the

Living One, Master of wind and waves, will surely come quickly for our salvation, even though it may be in the fourth watch of the night. See Matthew tells us Jesus came to the disciples "during the fourth watch of the night." In scripture the Romans divided the night into four different shifts. 6:00 p.m. – 9:00 p.m.; 9:00 p.m. – 12 midnight; 12 midnight – 3:00 a.m.; 3:00 a.m. – 6:00 a.m. But they had been in the boat since before sundown the previous day. Why did Jesus wait so long to save them?

If I were one of the disciples, I too would have preferred Jesus to show up "*immediately*" or ahead of the storm. I'd prefer Jesus to show up in an Amazon Prime or same day kind of delivery. Matthew wanted his readers to learn to wait. Another pivotal point to the story is waiting also involved Peter's decision to leave the boat. He didn't do this on the strength of his own impulse; he asked Jesus' permission first, and then waited for an answer. I wonder if another type of external waiting was involved for Peter.

In this chapter, I want you to think about this, before you add to your cart. I want you to think about Peter, and this activity that Peter and the other disciples had to engage in right up to the very end: Waiting. You're now trusting God; you hop out of the boat. You take a step of faith – you bravely totally boss babe courageously choose to leave a comfortable job to devote yourself to Gods calling; you will use a gift you believe God has given you even though you are scared to death; you will take relational risks even though you hate rejection; you will go back to school even though people tell you it is too late, or it doesn't make sense financially; you decide to trust God and step up and step out.

Well maybe you will experience instant gratification, or immediate confirmation that your decision was correct and you'll be crowned with victory and success. You will grow spiritually and life will be thriving, your faith is stronger than ever, yes, all the good stuff. Your friends are proud of you, all in that beep-beep move moment. But what if errrkkk. … stop the car moment; it does not work out like that? What if we are still waiting? That job or next calling in your life didn't happen yet, you followed your calling and you're like, "Hello, ding dong God, it's me again, so I followed your plan! Here I am ready to live my best life!" and you don't hear anything in that moment. There is no monumental moment where the restoration is beginning. Walls are being built and painted and all that HGTV fun stuff that happens in sixty minutes. Yo Jesus, I umm got the contractor here ready to work? But you haven't told me what we're doing yet?

God does not always move at our pace and our minute. We are all jacked up, can I say jacked up? Well I did, we are all jacked up on double macchiato, skim milk, extra salted caramel latte. Let me take a selfie in my car #Livingmybestlife, when some of your friends are so broken, and say, "Wow, I wish I could live like that." Feeling not held up to the expectations I seem to present, little do they know I just spent the last three dollars in my bank account. What I am trying to say is that we are all going too fast. We're not enjoying the season of waiting. Every one of us, doesn't matter if we're a pastor, teacher, student, wife, mother or father, we will experience waiting and will have to learn to wait at some point of time in your life. "But God, I just healed from my past, I am ready to conquer the world. God, look at me I am ready to receive my best life!" I started a blog, I started journaling. All of those things are exceptional, I did it. Took me over five years but I did. Waiting for your purpose is the single hardest thing we are called to do. So sometimes it is frustrating to turn to the Bible and find that God himself, who is all powerful and all wise, keeps saying to his people, *Wait.* "Be still before the Lord, and wait patiently for him ... Wait for the Lord, and keep to his way, and he shall exalt thee to inherit the land." Forty-three times in the Old Testament alone, the people are commanded to, "Wait. Wait on the Lord."

Waiting takes unseen hope. Waiting is not glamourous or easy. Waiting is, by nature something only the humble can do with a whole lot of grace. It reminds us that we are not in charge. Most of you were stuck at home for a period of time home schooling during the COVID-19 virus. I know my family and I did a whole lot of waiting. Waiting humbled me in ways I needed to be humbled. But when it comes to life, we are not just waiting around – we're waiting on God. Therefore, we can trust his wisdom and timing. We can wait with passion. We can wait with purpose because we know his plan is better than ours. We can wait with boldness because we are confident. Waiting reminds us that we are waiting for someone; the single most important activity in *waiting* is *prayer.*

I remember waiting for a job as a Nurse five years ago when I was laid off from my last hospital. It was due to budget cuts. I still remain friends with most of that staff and nurses. It wasn't personal, it was business. I loved that hospital. It broke my heart. But I had to learn a lesson in waiting. I didn't feel qualified anymore. I lost my calling. I was employed at that hospital for many years; I had lost all confidence after I was laid off. It was about five years ago, I was applying and frantically looking for jobs. I had just met my husband at the time. I was newly married; and boom I didn't have a job. I thought what a failure I am. He was the man of my dreams, most of the time (insert laughing with tears emoji) but seriously it was the best, healthiest relationship I ever had. So I was started job searching on a poplar job site. I applied for a job that required higher qualifications than my nursing license. I was hired as a Nurse Liaison, which was a Registered Nurse position and I was a Licensed Practical Nurse for which I felt unqualified. I applied because I wanted to be a part of a major national rehab hospital so I could develop big boy corporate data analysis marketing skills and further my clinical knowledge. Imagine my shock when I found out I was hired for which I had no Bachelor's or another four year degree. I remember hitting my knees when I got the call. I praised Jesus. I was excited and terrified all at the same time.

But then I immediately became anxious, worrying, doubting myself. Honestly, I was front row, roller coaster terrified. The tasks we needed to complete were things I had never done before on such a big corporate level. How was I going to compete in the market alongside such educated colleagues with professional certifications and extra credentials? Imagine me rolling up, "Hey y'all, my mom used to say fake it till ya make it." Here I am. But I was not giving myself any grace. I wasn't trusting God. I was silently fighting the lie in my head that I was not good enough. Here came all the old issues and chains that tried to take over my mind. You're not good enough, you're not at home with your children, you're not at home cooking dinner for your family, and you're not a good mother. You will never write that book, who do you think you are writing a book? You have social media as a platform, and everyone can speak now. I was really awful to myself. I was not walking on what my life's purpose was. No one was knocking down my door or ringing my phone off the hook because they wanted me. I had to shut those lies over my life that were trying to block the purpose of my life. The enemy will use whatever he can that will inhibit Gods calling over your life.

I ended up getting the job and have been employed there over four years now. During that season of *waiting,* and external restorations, I had to learn the humility in waiting. I had to humble myself. Have you ever found yourself anxiously waiting? Sometimes what we wait for is not more important than what happens to us while we are waiting. If you have ever felt like that, then you can relate to Gideon as well. In Judges 6 of the Bible, we find the Israelites are oppressed by another nation, yet again, because of disobedience. They began crying out to God. He selected and called Gideon to be the deliverer of His people.

Gideon was so afraid of the situation they were in that he hid. God sent an Angel to Gideon who addresses him as Mighty Warrior. Gideon was not excited about the way he was addressed. Not only does he say he is the least in his family, but he also begins a rant; telling the angel all of his concerns and venting all of his anger. After the back and forth between the two and the very apparent disbelief in his abilities, Gideon finally consents to be the deliverer after asking for many signs to make sure God is calling him. It is a great story of one person confronting and dealing with their anger, doubts, and fears. It is a story of one person who decided to do it ANYWAY! I encourage you to read the story in its entirety. (Judges 6-8). There is so much we can learn from Gideon's story. I will talk about three lessons we can learn from Gideon that will help you gain or re-gain your confidence so that you can achieve what you have been selected to do even though the external restoration hasn't happened yet and you're waiting. You may be doubting your ability. You may feel unqualified and not worthy but God takes the unqualified and qualifies the called.

Here are three things you can do to feel confident during restoration:

1. We Must Renew our Mind.

When Gideon started his conversation, there were so many doubts. However, by the end of his conversation, we find Gideon in a posture of worship. Judges 6:19-24 shows that Gideon renewed his mind. In verses 13-16, Gideon was doubting not only himself but God. However, as he continued talking with God and staying in His presence, laying his concerns before God, his mind was transforming. The internal restoration had begun. He asked God for a sign; God provided the sign and he moved out but not before building an altar. An altar is a place of sacrifice and worship, not just for weddings. Gideon's mind was renewed! A renewed mind creates a renewed strength, which in turn creates renewed courage (even if it starts out in the dark where no one can see it!) As you continue reading the story in Judges, you will find that Gideon went against his own family to obey God. Slight commercial break, do you remember that story of me pulling my Bible out of the trash, Gideon my man, Ok back to the story. The Ball and Asherah altars he destroyed belonged to his Father. After destroying them, he then built an altar to God on top of the destroyed altars! Another sign of worship. Yep, his mind was renewed! He went from questioning God to worshipping God.

2. We Must Pray

Gideon's mind was renewed and it happened with prayer. Remember prayer is the most important tool in waiting. Prayer changes things! It changes the situation. It changes the perspective. It changes the reaction! You go in one way (angry, scared, discouraged) but you come out another (peaceful, bold, with purpose, courageous, inspired, peaceful). In my option, Chapter 6 is one long prayer because prayer is a conversation with God, right?

When you pray without ceasing, you are aligning your heart and focus to the voice of God. You can hear God's commands and you act accordingly. Fervently praying during a time of restoration.

3. We Must Act and Trust.

As Gideon kept doing what God told him, God revealed more for him to do. He kept doing act after act after act. God was speaking and he was obeying. As he was obeying and doing what God told him, his trust was developing. Your trust can only develop as you go! Trust is built as you act. When you move God moves. As you continue to move, you continue to see God move in MIGHTY ways thereby increasing your trust in Him. I trust God to provide for me with the ninety percent because I tithe the ten percent, and He has! I trust God to go before me when I speak because when I speak he has given me a word. I trust God to give me an encouraging word to speak to women at conferences and expo's because when I follow up with them over the phone or meet a fellow sister for coffee and Jesus has done it over and over again. Women receiving breakthroughs. When God moves you see the miraculous things he does. You start saying, "Wow!" Your trust builds and it makes you step out there again. Let me encourage you my friend to neither wonder nor worry about whether or not you are qualified. Do not worry if you have not found your purpose. You have one. You are qualified. If you get the vision and if God speaks to you faithfully, follow it. He is a way maker. You are so much more than your circumstances.

"For I know the plans I have for you," declares the
LORD, "Plans to prosper you and not harm you, plans
to give you hope and a future."

(Jeremiah 29:11)

God restored a lost relationship with my biological mother on
a birthday of mine several years ago. My whole family and siblings
came over that did not happen for over four years.

"Trust in the LORD, with all your heart and lean not
on your own understanding; in all your ways submit
to him, and he will make your paths straight."

(Proverbs 3:5-6)

CHAPTER 6

Diversity and Difference

NOW WORKING ON THE RENEWED MIND, YOU HAVE been waiting and praying, and now re-aligning your focus and *Trusting* onto God and not your past and pain. How do you feel? All better? I wish I could tell you, "Yup, you can stop reading now, you're fixed. You are going to go on and never hurt again but I would be lying to you and as my mother said, "God don't like ugly." So I'm not going to lie. Healing is messy. Healing and using your story, your purpose to help others will bring you the most healing, other than God of course. I have my moments at times trying to go for a jog down Pity Ave. I have to keep that renewed mind and tell myself, "No, I am not going to allow the enemy to take me down old roads. God has new roads for me and although, those roads are uncharted and might seem a bit scary and new, I refuse to go back down Pity Ave and feeling sorry for myself."

Have you ever known someone from a blended family? Or are you from a blended family? I have always felt that blended families are something special. Different personalities, different opinions, different ideas, blending of holidays, traditions, expectations hopes and dreams but I always think coming from a blended family, I say blended and blessed because you have adapted. You have been given a bonus family member or maybe a bonus parent. You learn to *compromise*. It takes a person with a big heart to be or come from a blended family. They say blood is thicker than water, but I disagree. Some family, who is not blood, loves and treats you better than your blood family. When you are brought or have brought other children into the marriage it is a very vulnerable season. A lot of emotions flying around, we have walked some pretty hard moments having and raising a blended family. Raising a blended family requires a whole lot of love and an extra-large whole lot of grace. If you have a blended family, I highly recommend the book *The Smart Stepfamily* by Ron L. Deal. He is what I would call the Father of stepfamily education. The biggest take away I had after reading his book was *EXPECT DIFFICULTIES, THINK BIBLICALLY.*

How are the parents in a stepfamily affected by loss? Are you a stepparent? You also are facing many challenges. Your stepchildren often will not automatically love you, accept you, or respond to your discipline. It's also hard to be the biological parent in a stepfamily. It's tempting to try to buffer your own children from the effects of divorce and to deal with your guilt over the end of your marriage by being overly indulgent. As a result, your spouse can feel undermined as he or she tried to parent. If both of you have brought children into your marriage, this can create a corrosive atmosphere of "favorites" that splits the family into competing factions.

You might recognize some of these difficulties in your own blended family, and you can probably add your own personal particular blended family problems. But instead of being discouraged, know this: Difficulties are to be expected in a family living under the sun, we are not above it! Blended families don't simply represent two people coming together in marriage; each new stepfamily represents two worlds – Worlds of hopes, dreams, expectations, habits, traditions, personalities – coming together in a context of loss. Stepfamily difficulties don't mean that you or your family members are somehow deficient or are failures but they do mean you are going to have to restore your family and disciple as the Priesthood in your home.

My point I am piecing together for you is there will always be diversity and difference. I come from a very diverse, dynamic background. I have had to learn to adapt to make the best of my situation and so will you. I have had to learn and I am still learning to shut my mouth sometimes when people can be really ugly, and remember it is not my place to jerk a knot in someone's tail, shout out to my Southern's, ya'll know what I mean. There will always be a variety of opinions on how to live your life, what you should be doing, how you should be healing, and no one's voice matters except our ultimate healers, Jesus. I want you to pause, and double clap to that one for me, if anyone asks, tell them to kindly, "Worry 'bout ya self."

Sometimes you have to move back to move forward.

You have to step back and look at yourself, like the broken girl I was when I had to step back and look at myself in the mirror that day. Things will be different. There is a one hundred percent solid confirmation that you will not remain in a place of pain. God is the way, truth and light. It is not organically normal for you to remain in that state of pain in state of difference, our calling on our life is so much more than we could even imagine. God wants to use your story, your calling to bring others to salvation. Your story is unique, beautiful, sacred and He wants to plant you where you can bloom into the beautiful perfect person you are. You are made in His creation, not anything else.

We were made to be different, unlike to one another when standing next to your sister in Christ. We were born to develop, constantly growing closer to Him. I love a good book but there is no perfect self-help book. The ultimate 'Self-help' book is the Bible. We seek to glorify God through studying the word of Jesus. We are different when comparing one testimony to another but destined to take a test to a testimony. A mess into a message, a trial into a triumph, a victim into a victory!

There is no victory without a battle, and no miracle without an impossible circumstance. I want you to pause and read this scripture in Matthew 7:7-12 and then come back. Now, I want you to write on a sheet of paper, or in this book three things:

1. What are you asking in this test to become a testimony?

2. What are you seeking in this impossible circumstance to become a miracle?

3. What door are you knocking on to open in your life for a victory?

Read this prayer out loud as a declaration of faith and vision:

Dear Father God, I (your name) desire to take hold of the vision you have for me and pray that you would lead and guide me to take a collective step of faith in the direction that You would have it go. Help me pray to grasp the vision that you have over my life and may I be sensitive to Your leading and guidance and not mine. Prevent me from seeking to implement my own inferior ideas, or substitute my own manmade notions for Your plan and purposes. Draw me closer to You as I seek Your face together in prayer. May I be strengthened in the inner women, united to you in the unity of the faith and prompted to carry out Your plans and purpose over my life to serve you. I pray that your vision emerges in my heart on your perfect timing, not mine, Holy Spirit what do you have for me to pick up and courageously face in this next Season? God, I want to see and believe that I am of enough value to be healed and to bring healing to others. Amen.

If you are in a place that this prayer doesn't apply to you, this is a perfect time to think about someone who might be in that place, and pray over them aloud. Pick up the phone and call that person whom might be walking this out. Send them a text, email, Imessage or if you are not left handed like me, a hand written note would be even more personable.

CHAPTER 7

Comfort Zone

ARE YOU BELIEVING THE TRUTH ABOUT YOUR LIFE OR the lies of doubt? If you've ever asked any of these questions, I want you to know, you can walk confidently in your calling even when you feel unqualified. Yes, even when you have a million reasons for why you're not good enough. Even if you're not entirely sure what it is. Can we look at Moses as he is really applicable for the woman who feels unqualified to walk in her calling? So pull up a chair, this is a good one. Can you tell yet, I am actually getting better at my grammar and punctuation ha!

Moses Felt Unqualified to Walk in his calling. I can relate to Moses. The Bible says he had a stutter and felt like he couldn't speak well, let alone command a whole Pharaoh to let God's people go. I can relate because I struggle with social anxiety and being in social settings typically makes me uncomfortable. I try to be funny or loud to overcompensate my insecurity by coming off secure. Most of the time, it works. People find me funny and laid back. Some people find me annoying. But every time I leave a gathering, I re-play the scenarios and think about if anyone liked me or not. I'm not exaggerating when I say this: When I was little I always wanted to be friends with the popular girls and the pretty girls.

I never felt good enough. Even in my grown years, I still find the enemy trying to drag me down. To fill me with doubt and anxiety. When I am in a gathering of very successful, smart, educated people, I say to myself, "How did I get here?" I am not qualified to be around these people. BUT I am, I have to deliberately make a decision right there! Are you going to believe the enemy that came to give you a spirit of doubt? Or are you going to be believe Truth! The truth is you are worthy, qualified and good enough.

What I learned from the life of Moses is that **God doesn't call the qualified, he qualifies the called. "Moses knew that anything he was going to accomplish for these people had to come from God, because in himself, Moses could accomplish nothing."** That's the thing. When you feel unqualified, you're in a better position than the people who believe they have it all together because if done the right way, you see God as your ultimate source and you recognize that you really can't do it on your own.

What if I don't know exactly what my calling is or where God is leading me? When God called Moses, he told him to speak to Pharaoh and free the people. Moses had no idea that he would eventually become the leader of a growing nation! You might not know where God is leading you but walking in your calling is not always about having a specific destination–it's about choosing to go wherever God wants you to.

Here are three tips to help you get out of your comfort zone:

1. Walk in God's Timing, Not Your Own:

    "God moves in his timing, not yours. He's never late, but He is usually not early either." God called Moses to set the Israelites free but he didn't just send him out right away. There was a long period of preparation where Moses wasn't even in Egypt. You might not feel qualified when God calls you but don't worry about that. All you need to do is be open to him preparing you; he does a pretty good job at that. The waiting season is never usually easy. It comes with a lot of struggle and sometimes a lot of pain but it's worth it if you want to grow into the woman God is calling you to be. God might have given you an amazing dream but sometimes he'll have you wait before sharing it with the world. That's because he wants to grow and develop the dream so that when it's out there, it's as impactful as it was meant to be.

2. **"Go for No":**

    "Yes is a destination, No is how you get here." **Failing and failure are two different things. Unfortunately, you're bound to experience**

rejection or hear the word "no" a few times if you're called. Don't let rejection make you feel like you weren't called in the first place. Pharaoh rejected Moses' request many times. He refused to let the people go. That doesn't mean that Moses wasn't called. In the same way, just because people reject you or don't like what you're doing doesn't mean that you're not called. *"We are not trying to impress the world with what we are offering because we are not offering a product or experience, but rather, we are giving a message; the only message!* Simply put, you're not here to impress anyone. You're here to follow Jesus as he leads you. People may not be impressed but as long as God is pleased, you're okay.

3. **Go Deep with God – Even if you have to go alone:**

   "When it comes to the called, you will never be able to give and teach what you yourself haven't been given by God." This next point is solid gold. It's so important to spend time with God because he is our source. He's the one who fills us up. If you feel unqualified, go to him. He'll give you exactly what you need to accomplish the purpose he has for you. You can't pour from an empty cup, so if you don't go to God for constant refreshing, you'll always feel unqualified. Spend time in his presence and get to

know his heart. Sometimes it'll be alone, that's okay. God calls anyone he wants to. The Bible says he's no respecter of persons. So, if you're reading this feeling like, "No this couldn't possibly apply to me," prayerfully reconsider. Maybe God led you to this book for a reason.

Go wash your hair, if you're feeling extra stressful and full of emotions blow dry it. Style it, you will feel better, trust me! Walk around in your robe, the nice one that your Aunt gifted you. Look in the mirror and tell yourself you are beautiful. Who cares what people think about you? Who cares what the neighbors are doing? You are alive, you are breathing, and you have food in your fridge. Go pull out that ice cream. Go to bed early; get a good night's rest. Wake up early have that coffee and watch the sun rise. You are called for something big. Something great but you have to get out of your comfort zone.

CHAPTER 8

Cancer on the First

SO NOW THAT I HAD COMBATED, FACED, SPEAR-headed every major issue and circumstance that was very hard for me not to hide any more in grief, this is the moment I was beginning to feel that I had developed a very good pace for my life. I had survived and overcome two divorces. The children were adjusting to their new home, new school, and we were doing I would say fairly well. Sure, we still had our own family chaos and sorts of charades that come with being in a blended family, busy schedules and agendas with sports, piano, chess but overall life was pretty good. We went to church on Sundays, and gathered around the dinner table at least once or twice a week given no baseball practice. I felt like things had finally settled down for me. My mother was still not speaking to me for her issues. I have no idea, I could sneeze wrong and she would complain to everyone about it and she would make sure everyone knew about it but I was in a pretty good place and didn't seem to take it personally anymore.

That part of me had healed, and I realized that I did not have to carry her issues anymore. Did it still hurt? Yes. Did I want to call and tell her how I really felt? Absolutely. But something in the past few years spoke deep to me. It wasn't my place or my job. I would have gladly volunteered, believe me! She used to tell my siblings she's only trying to be nice because she is a 'Christian.' I laughed and said, "Probably, otherwise I may have not been so quiet."

However, I had an open and active relationship with my biological mother. It somewhat filled a void for me, for the adult daughter, but that little lonely girl still longed for that relationship with her Mom, the one who had raised her. I wanted so much for her to hold me in her arms, or to French braid my hair. To go for a drive to her favorite ice cream shop on the beach and get a drive-through cone. Or to drink a black stale cup of coffee, and sit on the couch and watch her favorite HGTV show that she has already seen ten times, and talk about all the house remodels she was in the middle of doing. She had such a knack for envisioning what is and what could be. But it was sad she could never see what could be with us. It was a lesson I had already known was so easy in the palm of her hands and could be restored. Painfully, it was not my lesson to teach. I begged God, "Jesus, listen you are the way maker, can't you lend a hand here and restore this?" I just learned to put it in my pocket, and hang onto the few good memories we had. When I missed her I would pull those joyful moments out of my pocket, enjoy them, and tuck them carefully back in my pocket. Cherished and safe.

Not even she could remove those. Then I received some wonderful news, a new outlook on life. I learned that I was expecting in November 2018. I waited for almost a good month, before I told my husband as we suffered a miscarriage at fourteen weeks eight months prior. I deep down was longing for a little girl. All of my friends and family could tell you in a Miami hot minute I was praying for a precious beautiful baby girl. I was praying that I wanted to be the mother to a daughter I had never had. I had two mothers but one pushed me so far away. I forgot what our home used to smell like. My biological mother lived over two thousand seven hundred and fifty miles away. Yes, I checked it on MapQuest. We had visited a few times and it was nice to learn my family history and roots but it always came with a bitter taste as it reminded me of a broken relationship and trying to figure out where I fell into that loyalty. She did the best she could to accommodate me but no matter how much I tried to force this new foreign love it never felt home to me. She is genuine, southern and "Bless your heart" through and through, and a believer but I still had to re-learn that, especially being all grown up and not a child anymore. I had to stop controlling how I feel and let old wounds heal. I had to remain abided in His Love. (John 15:1-17). I was content where God had cut some branches off that were not bearing fruit. Keep pressing, keep walking, keep continuing. I stopped holding myself to this expectation that I had to have it all figured out. A good friend of mine was the only one to know before anyone that I was expecting. She was so elated for us. I gave my husband a Christmas card a few weeks before Christmas and it said, "Your gift this year is only small but will take up a lot of room in your heart. Baby Miller, Due July 2019." He cried and asked how long I knew. I told him I just wanted to be sure this time. It was the best Christmas. It felt complete and whole. I never had a gender reveal party for my two boys; that really was not a thing back then. It was January, Morgan and I secretly knew the gender of the baby we were having and jumping with joy to share with our family. Everyone had made their guesses. Cutting into the cake, everyone's face on edge, leaning forward enough to grab the first glimpse of shade of frosting on the cake knife. Would it be pink or blue? The family goes wild. Baby pink icing coated the cake knife. We cried so overfilled with a prayer we had been praying for years. Eight months earlier a prayer we thought would not be fulfilled. We stayed faithful, we stayed happy either way. God would have decided to bless us, that we would not be with a heart of discernment but blessed with every moment he gave us. I could finally be the mother to a precious baby girl I had dreamed and thought. Everything was going well. I had no complications, she was healthy and growing. Loving my boys as I was a #Boymom first, they will always be my fun, energetic, spunky, rough and rowdy boys, dirty socks and clothes all over the house, picking up loose bullets from dart guns on the ceiling fan boys but I felt like that lost little girl was no longer lost.

March 2019, Phone rings. It's one of my siblings. She received a call that Mom was not doing so well and needed her to come over the next day. She asked me to come as I was not the only one on the 'outs' in the family. We met, picked up her favorite meal, and brought it to her. Nothing would prepare me for what I was going to see. Now reminding you, I am a Nurse for over nine years now. She had some new onset of issues that she never had before. I knew deep down after my own personal nursing assessment it was something much bigger than the family was ever prepared to take on. I told my Mom my advice and she kindly shot it down as if I was inflating the situation and diagnosis. We ended up making a deal, she was to go to the emergency room the next day as she was a Registered Nurse and very verbal about her own care. I promise out of all my years of nursing, nurses make the worst patients. I agree because I am a terrible patient as well.

My sister and I stepped outside. I desperately needed fresh air, and she was right behind me clinging on to any body language signs I was giving off that she could try to interpret. It was bad, I was mentally talking to myself, "Give her something delicately," so I would share a breadcrumb. I will give her credit as she is mature beyond her years. She suspected and was trying to confirm with me. We left that evening shaken from our very core that no one is invincible. I did not grow up in a hugger family; we did not tell each other "Love you" with goodbyes. That night my sister and I hugged and said we loved each other. I drove home with the windows down, the cold air slapping me in the face the reality I was just faced with. So many thoughts I had flying through my head. I was still wearing the nursing hat, processing, analyzing, my brain going one thousand miles a minute, contacts, old connections to pull in, like a Navy ship going out for deployment, reaching and grasping mentality to the reserves. I went home that night and just poured out to my husband. His face, a really good poker face, prepared because I could see it in his eyes. He had been through this before, but he was just quietly picking up all my emotions flying at him and piecing me back together.

I woke up bright and early with an agenda. My Type A personality was ready to work, and problem solve, and get this deployment underway. My brother helped me the next morning. I washed my Mother gently and brushed her hair. My Mom was glad I was there but I was internally an emotional wreck. I had come flooding back into her life, but I was there to help my sister. No phone call reconciliation. I was there telling her she was going to be ok. We would get her pain medication adjusted and started a load of laundry for her before we left. I thought, "Aren't we supposed to hug this out? Aren't we going to discuss things?" But the words couldn't pour out of me like I had thought they would. I memorized a dialogue for when this moment would present itself as I had gone over this in my head thousands of times. But it was not the narrative I had captured in my head.

"We're here Mom. Let me get a wheelchair to help you out of the car." An old pal of mine, in the emergency room, who helped get things moving along.

Knock at the door. "Yes, come in." I was still wearing my white coat.

"Are you the daughter?" The doctor asks.

I am lost and adrift and not really sure what to say or not to say at the moment. My mom responded, "Yes." My cheeks became flushed as that was the first confirmation I had received in over four years. Ok I didn't imagine reconciliation in a hospital emergency department, but okay.

"Young Lady, can we take a walk?" Well it wasn't her, so I figured he was speaking to me and I nodded.

We walked down the hall; I could tell my suspicions were correct from the body language of the doctor. The doctor was wearing his cheaters low on his nose, his shoulders dropped over, wiping his brow with his left hand, and holding the records in the right. He asked some residents to move, and brought me into the doctor's dictation area. (That is where all the doctors chart and do their work.)

"Now, I am about to show you some things. Can you tell me what this is?"

I acknowledged what I saw, and interpreted and asked for verification.

He said, "Ok, good."

I think he was feeling me out for what he was about to drop.

He said, "Ok, come with me."

We start walking back, and he paused. "Aimee, I am about to drop a nuclear bomb on you and your family, and I am going to need you to be really strong for your Mom."

I grabbed the handrail, bracing for the blow.

"Your Mom has Cancer Metastasis, but we don't know the source. Usually, when it spreads to the bone, its terminal."

"It's in every vertebra in her body."

I hit my knees, lip curling, tears flowing, and trying to grab onto any last strength I had to get it together. I could not. I was broken.

He gave me a few minutes, and put his hand on my shoulder, and said, "I am so sorry." He notified some staff and it was all hands on deck. Everyone was so nice, and it was like watching a movie that I did not sign up to play in. Everything had slowed down around me.

He said, "Young lady, I am going to need you to be really strong right now. We're going to go in and give your Mom the news. I want you to hold her hand, and try not to cry, but smile. We are going to try to rear its ugly head."

We walked, I after him. I walked into the room and stood beside my Mother. Picked up her left hand and placed it in mine. She knew. She looked at me with her best nurse smile, and I tried with every ounce of strength down to the pit of my stomach to not shed a tear. My glasses fogged up, wiping my tears away stained with my foundation and mascara.

"So Ma'am, we kind of know what's going on. We know that this is Cancer, and that it has spread but we don't know where it is coming from. Do you have any idea where this could have started? Any family history?"

She responded with, "It's Breast Cancer."

My eyes could not hold back the pressure of water flooding like a damn. The flood broke, tears pouring out. Standing stiff, to lock my knees from giving out, trembling. I kept holding her hand safe in mine. I told her we were going to beat it, and if I knew anyone as stubborn and strong as she, she could beat it.

She stated that she had felt a lump, and didn't want to investigate it as she feared she knew what it was. She was the strength of the family, the matriarch of her domain. She did not have time to pause and be weak and do self-care. It was Terminal Breast Cancer Metastasis Stage Four. It wasn't a diagnosis that a lost daughter or anyone for that matter wanted to hear at that point. They went on with tests, and Mom had asked me to call the children and let them know. It was too many phone calls I had to make and re-live the worst moments in my life over and over and over and over and over again.

After I pulled myself together off the lawn of the hospital, leaning on the oak tree to hold me up, I had to re-collect myself and go back into the hospital. It was after a few weeks that my

Mom was able to go home with a new aggressive treatment plan. My siblings and I had to adjust to this new painful season. We did our best to put up a performance and a strong face in front of our Mom. Taking shifts and turns, all participating in every way we could. It was probably the most time my family and I had spent together in these unfortunate circumstances. I had put on my shield of faith.

> [10] Finally, be strong in the Lord and in his mighty power. [11] Put on the full armor of God, so that you can take your stand against the devil's schemes. [12] For our struggle is not against flesh and blood, but against the rulers, against the authorities, against the powers of this dark world and against the spiritual forces of evil in the heavenly realms. [13] Therefore put on the full armor of God, so that when the day of evil comes, you may be able to stand your ground, and after you have done everything, to stand. [14] Stand firm then, with the belt of truth buckled around your waist, with the breastplate of righteousness in place, [15] and with your feet fitted with the readiness that comes from the gospel of peace. [16] In addition to all this, take up the shield of faith, with which you can extinguish all the flaming arrows of the evil one. [17] Take the helmet of salvation and the sword of the Spirit, which is the word of God. [18] And pray in the Spirit on all occasions with all kinds of prayers and requests. With this in mind, be alert and always keep on praying for all

the Lord's people. [19] Pray also for me, that whenever I speak, words may be given me so that I will fearlessly make known the mystery of the gospel, [20] for which I am an ambassador in chains. Pray that I may declare it fearlessly, as I should.

(Ephesians 6:10-20)

I was depending on Gods strength and used every piece of his armor. The whole body needs to be armed just like in armor. Five months *pregnant*, and being a *caregiver to my Mom* was not where I thought I would be. *She* followed aggressive treatment plans, and a strategic plan to fight and beat this incurable Cancer. I hate that word. Out of all my years of nursing I was naive enough to say that it never bothered me personally because I knew the stages, I knew the treatments, I was comfortable and pretty well versed in it. My Mom was an Oncology/Cancer Nurse for years, so I think as a teenager it didn't affect me because she would talk to us about it. It was a cold, ugly elephant in the room word.

I couldn't grieve the situation because I was in fear of a miscarriage due to all the stress that *not only* me *but my whole family was dealing with. It was a very tough time for all of us to try and digest* the situation. *How do you deal with that? How do you mentally put on a smile and be happy going to your OB-GYN doctor's appointment and hear a beautiful heartbeat and then drive to you*r *now mothers house to be her caretaker? It was the most appalling time being pregnant, and talking with her about her next radiation and chemotherapy session. Sweeping the hair* *up off the floor so she doesn't see it. A friend of mine, who was so thoughtful and aware, probably more than* me *at the time, gifted her with a beautiful bag full of silk, satin and head scarfs. Her favorite one was this aqua and pink one with I think palm trees. She loved everything and anything tropical. The more neon and seafoam the better. By then she started to lose a lot of weight. She went through some surgery to stabilize things and was doing quite well considering the doom and gloom news she had received months before. Walking, and checking her mail, sitting out by the pool, and sunbathing her legs. It was the first time we felt a sense of fresh air. Was this going to be okay? She would put her eyeliner on in the morning, and sit up in the living room* back *to watching those darn HGTV shows. It was nice to feel somewhat normal for the time being.*

It was a time that fear was to be stopped in its tracks. It was a time to exhale and regroup.

How do you combat fear? How do we cut the ropes of worry in which we may find ourselves in a storm?

Matthew 6:25-33 tells us not to worry because we are valuable in Gods Sight:

> [25] "Therefore I tell you, do not worry about your life, what you will eat or drink; or about your body, what you will wear. Is not life more than food, and the body more than clothes? [26] Look at the birds of the air; they do not sow or reap or store away in barns, and yet your

heavenly Father feeds them. Are you not much more valuable than they? ²⁷ Can any one of you by worrying add a single hour to your life?" ²⁸ "And why do you worry about clothes? See how the flowers of the field grow. They do not labor or spin. ²⁹ Yet I tell you that not even Solomon in all his splendor was dressed like one of these. ³⁰ If that is how God clothes the grass of the field, which is here today and tomorrow is thrown into the fire, will he not much more clothe you—you of little faith? ³¹ So do not worry, saying, 'What shall we eat?' or 'What shall we drink?' or 'What shall we wear?' ³² For the pagans run after all these things, and your heavenly Father knows that you need them. ³³ But seek first his kingdom and his righteousness, and all these things will be given to you as well."

Little did we know that we were in a storm each in different boats through uncharted waters. Gods overwhelming, abundant love for us meets our every need. When we begin to recognize this and understand more of our identity purpose in God, worry and fear begin to fall to the wayside. Worry leads to a striving life of self-preservation instead of one of resting in the unfailing love of God. When we seek Him first, we are rewarded with Him; He is the ultimate healer. When we refuse to be afraid of our destiny, we reap the confidence Jesus had intended for us.

Never let your fear confront your future.

A few months prior in the hospital, before returning home, a good friend of mine who owned a hair salon offered to cut her hair during her first hospital stay. The radiation and chemo was intense. I felt lucky to have such a sweet friend, who not only volunteered her time and skill, but also did so much more. We served together at our church and prayer altar team. I confided in her that my mom wasn't a believer and what I feared most was not restoring the relationship because, to be honest, it was never going to be the same. However, I wanted my Mom to find salvation more than anything else in this world. I wanted her to be prepared. I wanted her to accept Jesus Christ as her Lord and Savior. I knew time was of the essence. I prayed fervently for her every night.

My dear friend met me at this hospital, and cut my mother's hair. Gently we rolled her from side to side, and my friend carefully washed, blow dried and trimmed my mother's delicate hair. My friend said that if she felt God speaking to her, she would ask my Mom if she knew Jesus. My Mom was so thankful for the simple things – A fresh wash and cut. She laughed and said that she felt somewhat back to normal. So my sweet friend who I will not name, asked my Mom if she knew who Jesus was. Mother smiled and half cackled, "Yes." She then started to speak with her, and I felt maybe I should leave the room. This is a personal decision and I did not want to interject myself. I thought, "This is the woman who threw my Bible in the trash. This conversation could go one or two ways." My nerves were on the edge. I was just riding the conversation out, hoping it would not hit any personal waves or crash against the shore like a great big gust of wind.

To my surprise, the conversation went very smoothly. She allowed my dear friend to invite the Holy Spirit in the room. She prayed over my mother. I held one of my mother hands and my friend held the other.

My friend asked her, "Do you accept Jesus Christ as your Lord and Savior, that He died on the cross as a covenant to forgive us of our sins?"

My mother with her eyes closed, nodded and spoke, "Yes."

My friend spoke the most beautiful prayer over her.

I cried. I never thought I would see this day. She accepted Jesus as her Lord and Savior. It also scared me. I knew she was making her peace with the Ultimate Healer; I was so overwhelmed for her, thinking I would get her a Bible. But it was a confirmation for what was destined. A silent Bell.

I walked out of the room with my friend down the hall, hugging her and thanking her. Pulling the little hairs still stuck to her shirt from the fresh trim. She told me she was honored. So selfless, she did it with the most sincere God led heart. You don't meet those kinds of people. They are the real deal. No judgment, no opinions, just a whole lot of compassion in her heart to give. I will always love you my friend.

One night after caring for my mother all day, I was mentally and emotionally exhausted. I managed to draw up the energy to take a shower that night and put on a comfy robe that I knew would not fit much longer as my sweet baby girl was growing every day, and by the sign I almost couldn't see my toes was affirmation. I sat on the couch, made some tea, while everyone was sound asleep. I remember putting the song on, "Tell your Heart to beat again" by Danny Gokey. I was broken. I was so angry that she was slipping. I cried and cried every night. It was such a long day. The days were long, one after another. They began to run together. Working full-time as a Nurse, being five months pregnant, and caregiving for my family and looking after my mother, as well as being a mom to my other two children, and a wife, I was neglecting my family. It was at their dispense that was I was able to care for my mother. My husband understood. Leaving a left over plate wrapped with saran wrap in the refrigerator.

I was devastated. I had mentally prepared myself that my mother and I didn't have a relationship but she was still going to be there off in the distance. Not gone. Not of this earth anymore. I cried for hours, and hours, begging God not to take her. That she had just found salvation. That it wasn't her time to go. That she was just getting started. I knew it wasn't my lesson to teach but I let God know how I felt that night. I begged, pleaded and yelled. After hours of sobbing on the couch, my knees on the rug, curled over hugging the couch with my head buried in my arms; my husband came over and picked me up gently to my feet. He kissed my forehead and told me it was time to go to bed and rest.

He placed his hand on my belly and said she needs rest too. I slept in that morning, drinking a coffee, with a sobering mind of dried up tears that it was a realization I was going to have to deal with. Grief does not ask for your permission. I didn't speak for hours, still in shock of what was to come.

Until then

I wish I could say that she is healed and doing well here with us today, but I cannot. She held on and lived her best life until the very end. She hung on fearlessly more than I ever saw anyone fight in my nine years of nursing. In the end there was nothing neither I nor anyone else could do. It spread to her liver, and she did not want to tell us until she could not hide it anymore. She was a very good nurse. She put on a great face burying her issues to not affect us, although they did. We all tried to absorb those issues to give her a fighting chance. But in the end, she wanted her dignity and no one was going to take it. She passed away ten months later from the day she was diagnosed, Cancer on the first. She was with her children at the time and went peacefully.

I knew that she was in a better place. I was at work that day; the family had just called hospice two days prior. I received the call while at a work, in a meeting. I left as quickly as I could but did not make it in time. My other two siblings were there. I said a prayer over her and read Psalm 23. It was the hardest prayer I ever had to read aloud. My voice trembling, my heart felt like it was skipping beats, trying to turn my nursing hat on to suck it up and pull it together but I couldn't. I knew though, that she was in the house of the Lord forever.

CHAPTER 9

Spiritual Bassinet

THE SEASONS PAST, SLOWLY ADAPTING TO PREPARING for our new addition to the family. We went on, trying not to talk about the devastating loss to our family we had suffered. We kept busy by doing new projects, baseball, and my eldest perpetual love for fishing. I looked happy on the outside. A glowing expecting mother, doing the usual grocery shopping, and stopping at my favorite local guilty pleasure crème de la Cocoa on the weekends. I felt like I was being held together by the finest most detailed cotton so woven together it would take a special eye to see all the detail and specific fabric woven into perfect place. Where each thread of cotton supported the other. My sisters played a huge part in that. Each one holding up one other. We became so close as we were in our younger years, each one supporting and lifting one another when the other one was weak. You see, we weren't all strong at the same time, it came in waves. Each one riding out the wave and catching the other, like a well waxed surf board. Supporting the grip for the ride. It truly was a bond no one could break. We talked every day, and still do. We Facetime, Messenger, and all of us sisters are on a hilarious, raw Group Text. Sometimes we have a good day and sometimes we don't. But we have each other. It is a bond that I cannot compare to any other. We do life together, messy, fussy babies, upset, angry, intrigued by life. But at the end of the day, each one of us carries a small piece of the woman who raised us inside of one another. We find warmth in one another, four different personalities meshed with one another. Most of the time it is a good mesh; sometimes I am abrasive naturally as much as I try to reserve it, it comes out here and there. But we're authentically ourselves. I went many years lacking that relationship with my sisters and I don't think I could ever bare that again. They were a spiritual bassinet to me. It helped me grieve and heal. Each day, a new day, filled with laughter and support. A safe space to be protected from harm. My sisters were and are my saving grace. A true reality, like thunder lightening up the room and being woken up from the night thunderstorm rolling in. They were there. Whether you have sisters or a strong support system or not, God is there much more if you just ask Him. His is a presence you cannot deny. Maybe you're new to this walk; all you have to do is invite him in. Like a newborn baby tucked safely in a bassinet. You are clothed, covered, consumed in a spiritual bassinet. Safely in your Father's arms. Wrapped so delicately, like a muslins baby's blanket, tucking in all the parts. God is your spiritual bassinet. Built out of the sturdiest parts, you were created in His image. Secure, weathered and abled to stand the course. Recognize; acknowledge that you were given a special gift that no one can take from you no matter your pain, past or trauma.

"I can do all this through him who gives me strength."

(Philippians 4:13)

Are you content in any circumstances you face? Paul knew how to be content whether he had plenty or whether he was in need. The secret was drawing on Christ's power for strength. Do you have great needs, or are you discontented because you don't have what you want? Learn to rely on God's promises and Christ's power to help you be content. If you always want more, ask God to remove that desire and teach you contentment in every circumstance. He will supply all your needs, but in a way that he knows is best for you.

I am not saying I have all the answers but dwelling in a place of loss is not what God intended for you and me, my friend. Wake up and be thankful for what you have, pray for what you need, and have faith.

You have adapted your whole life. But what you call adaptation God calls admonition to warn you to turn from your weapon of choice to protect yourself from the enemy and choose truth. The truth that you are made in the fruit of the spirit.

[18] But if you are led by the Spirit, you are not under the law.

[19] The acts of the flesh are obvious: sexual immorality, impurity and debauchery;

[20] idolatry and witchcraft; hatred, discord, jealousy, fits of rage, selfish ambition, dissensions, factions [21]

and envy; drunkenness, orgies, and the like. I warn you, as I did before, that those who live like this will not inherit the kingdom of God.

²² But the fruit of the Spirit is love, joy, peace, forbearance, kindness, goodness, faithfulness, ²³ gentleness and self-control. Against such things there is no law.

²⁴ Those who belong to Christ Jesus have crucified the flesh with its passions and desires. ²⁵ Since we live by the Spirit, let us keep in step with the Spirit. ²⁶ Let us not become conceited, provoking and envying each other."

(Galatians 5:18-26)

Like a spiritual bassinet, if your desire is to have the qualities listed, then you must live with a renewed mindset. At the same time be careful not to confuse your subjective feelings with the Spirit's leading. Being led by the Holy Spirit involves the desire to hear, the readiness to obey God's word, and the sensitivity to discern between your feelings and his promptings. Live each day controlled and guided by the Holy Spirit. Then the words of Christ will be in your mind, the love of Christ will be behind your actions, and the power of Christ will help you control your selfish desires. There are two forces conflicting with us – the Holy Spirit and the sinful nature. Paul is not saying that these forces are equal – the Holy Spirit is infinitely stronger. But if we rely on our own wisdom, we will make wrong choices. If we try to follow the

Spirit by our own way to freedom from our evil desires, then that would be through the empowering of the Holy Spirit.

You have the means to see this through. You may or may not have a support system to walk this season through with you. Reach out to your church, small group, community support program. Love isn't supposed to hurt. You do not have to do life alone. Your setback, that painful time in your life doesn't mean *it won't* scar but it does mean it *will* heal. The story of Job is one of the literary classics in the Bible. It is a story that tries to sort out why bad things happen to good people. It is a story that tries to make sense out of the suffering. It is a story that concludes with an epic confrontation between Job and God. And it is a story that captures the isolation, the misunderstanding, and the feelings of abandonment.

Job's friends and his wife are convinced that it is Job's sin that has led to his misfortunes. That has a familiar ring to people trapped in violent and abusive relationships. "Why did you make him mad?" friends ask. "Why don't you just leave?" And inside the relationship the abuser often threatens even greater harm, if the victim tells anyone about what is happening. And if the victim decides to leave, the risk of violence increases, often with lethal consequences. As Job said of God, "If I go forward, he is not there; or backward, I cannot perceive him; on the left he hides, and I cannot behold him; I turn to the right, but I cannot see him ... If only I could vanish in darkness and thick darkness would cover my face!" (Job 23:8-9, 17)

Being a woman and a survivor of domestic violence – women often feel isolated, abandoned by family and friends who are uncomfortable or afraid of the topic, trapped by religious traditions that stress male dominance and the indissolubility of marriage and feel forgotten by God. Job knew that feeling. I have spent quite a bit of time in my past dealing with issues of domestic violence, particularly with the role of serving as a care partner in my church offering Christ like Care and being an advocate through friends and family on the topic. Over the last fifteen years, here in St. Augustine, I have lost two friends due to domestic violence. They were very tragic losses in the community. It seems to me that we in church communities have a special role in addressing domestic violence.

In far too many churches, abusers justify their violence by saying that wives are supposed to submit to their husbands. They apparently missed the next verse in the letter to the Colossians that says, "Husbands, love your wives and never treat them harshly" (3:19). The value that churches place on the sanctity of marriage can blind people to the undermining of marriage by violence. It is clinically documented that women who are religious have a higher chance of staying in a domestic violence relationship than a secular woman. Women are more often afraid to reach out.

Let's go back to Job for a minute. His life had taken a very bad turn. He tried to maintain his faith in God but it got harder and harder. Finally, he launches a powerful rant to God. He does not suffer in silence. He demands answers. Elie Wiesel, a Jewish writer who survived the Holocaust and knew at the core of his being what it is to suffer, wrote in his book *Reflection of Job* the following:

> "Once upon a time in a far-away land, there lived a legendary man, a just and generous man who, in his solitude and despair, found the courage to stand up to God. And to force Him to look at His creation."

People who feel abandoned by God, whether because of domestic violence or any other abuse should never feel alone. Never lose your faith in God. It is never your fault. It's about power and control. Power is absolutely central when thinking about issues of domestic violence. People who abuse and batter their partners are not simply losing their tempers. They are not simply having a bad day. They are seeking to exercise power and control over someone with whom they should be having a loving relationship. Remember those famous words from the apostle Paul?

> "Love is patient, love is kind; love is not envious or boastful or arrogant or rude. It does not insist on its own way; it is not irritable or resentful."

> (1 Corinthians 13:4-8)

Any one of us who have been in long-term loving relationships knows that there are days we are better at living that way than others. But people who physically and emotionally abuse their partners are not just having a bad day. They are using whatever tactics or weapons they have available—coercion and threats, intimidation or isolation, economic abuse or using children—to exercise power and control over their partner. None of these show up in Paul's list of what it means to love. None of these can be condoned by a faith community that claims to follow Jesus. None of these can be condoned by the wider society that seeks equity and justice.

You are loved. You are good enough. It is never too late. Find your group, find your people that you can weave into a tight night cotton blanket, supporting one another.

> [9] You, however, are not in the realm of the flesh but are in the realm of the Spirit, if indeed the Spirit of God lives in you. And if anyone does not have the Spirit of Christ, they do not belong to Christ.
>
> (Romans 8:9)

> [23] to be made new in the attitude of your minds; [24] and to put on the new self, created to be like God in true righteousness and holiness.
>
> (Ephesians 4:23, 24)

> [3] For you died, and your life is now hidden with Christ in God. [4] When Christ, who is your life, appears, then you also will appear with him in glory.
>
> [5] Put to death, therefore, whatever belongs to your earthly nature: sexual immorality, impurity, lust, evil desires and greed, which is idolatry. [6] Because of these, the wrath of God is coming. [7] You used to walk in

these ways, in the life you once lived. [8] But now you must also rid yourselves of all such things as these: anger, rage, malice, slander, and filthy language from your lips.

(Colossians 3:3-8)

The fruit of the Spirit is the spontaneous work of the Holy Spirit in us. The Spirit produces these character traits that are found in the nature of Christ. They are the by-product of Christ's control – we can't obtain them by trying to get them without his help. If we want the fruit of the Spirit to grow in us, we must join our lives to his. We must know him, love him, remember him, and imitate him. As a result, we will fulfill the intended purpose of the law – to love God and our neighbors, held safely in a Spiritual Bassinet.

Ask yourself these questions:

1. Which of these qualities do you want the spirit to wrap you up in a safe bassinet and produce in you?

2. In which areas of your life, do you need freedom?

3. Make a list, and find scripture to speak freedom over those.

CHAPTER 10

Courageously Guided

OK, I WILL ADMIT I AM TERRIBLE WITH DIRECTIONS. I need a point of reference to a place not an address or a road. So, by now you have read so far and we have unpacked a lot of content. We laughed and cried. I want to highlight some things so we can break it down even further. I want you to think of the last time you were courageous? Do you remember how you used Gods wisdom to help you? I want you to keep that in the back of your mind while you read.

What is the goal of the spiritual path? Freedom. Spiritual freedom is freedom from suffering caused by our pain. It is freedom from the suffering of the untrained instinctual body we all inhabit. It is the freedom and ability to live in peace. It is the freedom to choose how we engage with reality based on the present moment rather than previous beliefs and associations of our integrity. It is the freedom that comes from realizing that we and everything in us is free. This spiritual freedom is powerful beyond anything most people can imagine and it is always right here within us. Yet, people don't see it or know what it is. So, this chapter is dedicated to explaining what spiritual freedom is and the path that we can take to abide in that with the Holy Spirit. Gaining Spiritual Freedom with help you receive Gods wisdom. You will no longer be in an emotional prison.

An Invitation to Experience Freedom in the Gospel

Christian freedom is priceless, because Christ paid a heavy price for our sake. Yet why do we still prefer to live in the shadows of our hurtful past and addictions? God can set us free from any circumstance that we are facing today. Anyone who has experienced a bondage of some form or another – be it addiction, legalism, rituals, depression, anger, foul mouth, or even physical and sexual abuse – can be free. These bondages cast a shadow into our broken soul, and only Jesus Christ promises an abundant and free life today. Our sinful life hinders our relationship with a Holy and Mighty God. Christian freedom is an invitation where you can freely choose to accept God's offer for your soul. **You are invited to experience this freedom of Gospel through the following: Freedom through the Son of God.** Deuteronomy 21:22-23 says that if anyone commits a crime, he is put to death by hanging on the tree. He is cursed by God. In Galatians 3:13 we see this command was fulfilled by Jesus who was cursed because He was the substitute for our sins and hung on the cross. Through Christ, we experience freedom because He took upon Himself all our bondages and curses. "And you will know the truth, and the truth will set you free." (John 8:32). Who is the Truth? Jesus is the way, the truth, and the life. (John 14:6).

When we truly come to know the Truth of the Gospel, then our spiritual eyes are opened to the error of our sinful ways. Romans 8:1-2, NIV says: "Therefore, there is now no condemnation for those who are in Christ Jesus, because through Christ Jesus the law of the Spirit who gives life has set you free *from the law of sin and death.*" The intervention of Christ on behalf of mankind has put an end to the bondage of sin and Satan. If Christ didn't resurrect from the dead, then the Gospel would be futile and we would be forever bound to hell. But Jesus rose up on the third day, and praise God He has set us FREE! So, what does God expect back from us?

Here is the second point.

Freedom Through Surrender

> "Jesus, take the wheel
> Take it from my hands
> 'Cause I can't do this on my own
> I'm letting go
> So give me one more chance
> And save me from this road I'm on
> Jesus, take the wheel …"

This amazing song by Carrie Underwood conveys what surrender means. We often do not like to relinquish the control in our own lives or the lives of the people we are with. Christ wants us to surrender our will, our desire to follow our own rules that are against God's Word. We know that the road we are traveling on right now can be disastrous, so we must invite God to take over the control of every area in our lives. The truth is that we are not even in control of our own breath and heartbeat.

> Many a times others will tell us that surrendering our lives to Christ means being a slave of God. It is true, but we are voluntarily choosing to be God's servants, as ones who serve God and not sin.

> (Exodus 21:5-6)

> Being a slave of righteousness, of God is not drudgery, because the result will be holiness and eternal life.

> (Romans 6:22)

Paul, James, Peter and others proudly called themselves as 'bondservants of Christ.'

True spiritual freedom is where we deliberately decline the freedom to sin anymore. We must give up our desire to slander someone else or be a slave to lust.

2 Chronicles 7:14, says:

If my people, which are called by my name, shall humble themselves, and pray, and seek my face and turn from their wicked ways, then will I hear from heaven, and I will forgive their sin and will heal their land.

Because Christ overcame the grave, we can overcome any sin.

Freedom through Saving Grace

"Grace is free sovereign favor to the ill-deserving."

– B.B. Warfield

I believe grace is unmerited kindness extended to an undeserving person. We didn't deserve eternal life, or this amazing freedom in Christ, because of how unholy and sinful we've been. Yet, God saw it fit to redeem us and extend the hand of saving grace.

In Ephesians 2:8, NIV we read that, "For it is by grace are ye saved through faith – and that is not from yourselves, it is the gift of God."

The saving grace is completely God's gift to us through the work that was completed on the cross by Lord Jesus. It is about our spiritual salvation from sin secured by the covenant of grace where we are called children of God and His heirs.

For you have been called to live in freedom, my brothers and sisters. But don't use your freedom to satisfy your sinful nature. Instead, use your freedom to serve one another in love.

"God's grace grants us the freedom to do what is right, rather than to be slaves to what is wrong."

What is this Gospel of Freedom?

Gospel means "Good News," and the good news is that God offers to each mankind the forgiveness and victory over sin through His Son Lord Jesus Christ. The penalty of sin is death (Romans 6:23) and it pleased God to send His Only Son to take our wretched sin upon Himself and die on the Cross. (Romans 4:25). Christ died and rose again on the third day and claimed victory over death and sin. No other gods died and rose again for mankind. Now whosoever believeth on the Lord Jesus Christ and confesses her sins before God shall be forgiven of their sins. (Acts 4:12, Romans 10:9). My friend, God has given us a choice today. Choose to either experience freedom in the Gospel and be with Him in Heaven or to choose slavery to sin, eternal death, and the judgment of God.

Come to Jesus as you are, and vow never to turn back from God.

Ask yourself this?

The Bible says that where sin increases, Grace of God increases more. So, do you think we can continue to sin just because God's grace will continue to cover us?

Can we receive that level of forgiveness from Him? Can we forgive ourselves and others and leave the past in the past and move forward into a new future; one that doesn't need to be defined by any sort of evil or shame from our past? Can we have that same sort of mercy for ourselves and for others that our Father has for us already?

Freedom is not perfection. It's being open and pliable to the Holy Spirit to shape us and form us more and more into the image of our Father. Freedom is not a feeling or an event. It's a state of being. It's not passive or something that happens once and we're 'good to go.' It's actively pursuing our Father's heart and overcoming those areas in our life that are not from Him.

Freedom is no longer allowing the enemy to push us around but having a firm foundation established under our feet so that we can stand our ground against the enemy and overcome him. Freedom is being who you were created to be, the most normal you, who receives God's love and, in turn, loves God, loves oneself and loves others. Freedom is the joy of experiencing the unfeigned fruit of the spirit as it flows from your heart that has been made pure by the washing of the water of the Word. Freedom is the absence of bondage.

Freedom is a treasure to be pursued. Yet it is not something that just happens overnight. We have to grow up into it. God can strengthen us and mature us in it. We need to develop strength and endurance in this race. We may even run through different layers of freedom as we walk out of more and more bondage.

Therefore, since we are surrounded by such a great cloud of witnesses, let us throw off everything that hinders and the sin that so easily entangles. And let us run with perseverance the race marked out for us, [2] fixing our eyes on Jesus, the pioneer and perfecter of faith. For the joy set before him he endured the cross, scorning its shame, and sat down at the right hand of the throne of God. [3] Consider him who endured such opposition from sinners, so that you will not grow weary and lose heart.

(Hebrew 12:1-3)

So, sisters, will you choose in this moment to grab a hold of your Heavenly Father's hand and allow Him to lead you as a child so that you can grow up into this? If freedom is your desire, will you pursue His heart and His righteousness with your whole heart? Pray for wisdom.

The Creative Power of Prayer

Prayer is a tool essential for finding freedom. You know how they say that in our conversations with others we are either building up or tearing down? I was thinking about this in regard to our conversations with God. The beautiful thing about our interchange with the Father is that there is no tearing down, only building up.

Confess to one another, therefore, your faults (your slips, your false steps, your offenses, your sins) and pray [also] for one another, that you may be healed and restored [to a spiritual tone of mind and heart]. The earnest (heartfelt, continued) prayer of a righteous man makes tremendous power available [dynamic in its working].

(James 5:16 NIV)

Think about this. He is the Creator of all things. When we take things to Him concerning others, even concerning ourselves, where we might have a complaint or frustration, He hands us healing and forgiveness. Where we might bring Him dissatisfaction and disappointment, He meets us there with renewed vision and hope. If we enter His presence emptied of love, He pours out equally as extravagantly, filling us up all over again. In I Peter, the word says, His love covers a multitude of sins. In His presence, in prayer, that covers shortcomings and short-sighted views of ourselves and others too. When prayer is a continuous, unbroken means of expression between us and the Father, we can vent, we can war, we can wrestle, we can rest, we can hope and best of all, because of who He is, we can trust Him in intimacy.

Hebrews says He is the author and finisher of our faith. That means when we don't have the eyes to see our story to start with, we meet eye to eye with the originator of it. Even when we don't have faith for how things will end, with His power, He finishes perfectly.

We are assured and know that [God being a partner in their labor] all things work together and are [fitting into a plan] for good to and for those who love God and are called according to [His] design and purpose.

(Romans 8:28)

So, we don't have to have it all together to talk to Him. When we come to Him in prayer, we are operating in oneness with the Father, partnering and creating together. He has it all together. **We literally engage in partnership with the Father when we pray!** He owns all the deficit, all that we lack and all that we feel is missing. He's got it. He made us that way, not to frustrate us or leave us dissatisfied but to satisfy our longing *and* to satisfy His longing for communion and companionship with us! In prayer, we get renewed, recharged, we create our stories together and we reap endless rewards in His presence. There we thrive, in Prayer we thrive!

I know you have been hurt.

16 Therefore we do not lose heart. Though outwardly we are wasting away, yet inwardly we are being renewed day by day. 17 For our light and momentary troubles are achieving for us an eternal glory that far outweighs them all. 18 So we fix our eyes not on what is seen, but on what is unseen, since what is seen is temporary, but what is unseen is eternal.

(2 Corinthians 4:16-18 NIV)

We may never understand why we suffer. We MUST trust that God is good and sovereign. This should bring us joy and hope in our greatest times of need.

> ⁴ In all this you greatly rejoice, though now for a little while you may have had to suffer grief in all kinds of trials. ⁷ These have come so that the proven genuineness of your faith—of greater worth than gold, which perishes even though refined by fire—may result in praise, glory and honor when Jesus Christ is revealed.
>
> (1 Peter 1:6-7 NIV)

But you were made a warrior

Simplicity is about subtracting the obvious and adding the meaningful. You are a strong warrior. You are His bride. God will walk with you through this season. You have been hurt, but you are so much stronger than you know.

> For our rejoicing is this, the testimony of our conscience, that in simplicity and godly sincerity, not with fleshly wisdom, but by the grace of God, we have had our conversation in the world, and more abundantly to you-ward.
>
> (2 Corinthians 1:12)

Women warriors like things simple and perform at their best when it is simple. Simplicity creates a positive flow. Find your simplicity and embrace your strength. Simplicity is one of those things many people say they desire. Few actually live with simplicity. In my experience, there are two primary reasons why people tend to overcomplicate things. The first is a loss of focus. Many people tend to have no plan or direction in where they are going. Many seek all the various choices available to them. Where there is choice, there is complexity and misery. When you lose touch with why you are doing something, what you are doing, and where you are going, or when you begin chasing multiple things, you inadvertently sentence yourself to trivial pursuits and challenges. The next thing you know, you are lost or have created a life of chaos, challenges, and complexity.

A good example of loss of focus is chasing more than one rabbit at a time. You may chase them all; however, you will be unable to catch any of them. It is much easier to have clarity and focus on one.

> Therefore, since we are surrounded by such a huge crowd of witnesses to the life of faith, let us strip off every weight that slows us down, especially the sin that so easily trips us up. And let us run with endurance the race God has set before us.
>
> (Hebrews 12:1)

The key to having focus is having clarity. Where there is clarity, there is no choice. Where there is clarity, there is simplicity. Where there is simplicity, there is power. The other major reason we flock to complexity is a challenge of a very different nature. This requires a completely different solution. Society has rooted this in the ego. The ego's primary lubricant is summed up in one word: More. More stuff, more activities, more things, more money, more, more, more. We have become a 'more society.' The perception of the ego is that more is better, big is better than small, and less is just plain worse. More, more, more. This perception and behavior create more complexity and difficulty than required. The ego loves complexity and is induced by fear. Our ego relies on fear to protect itself, and complexity is a great place to hide behind.

The process of reaching an ideal state of simplicity at times may seem to be truly complex for you. The easiest way to achieve simplicity is through thoughtful reduction. When in doubt, just remove. Be sure you are congruent with what you choose to remove or reduce in your life. Warriors love to keep it simple.

Keep it clear. Think before you act. Many complications arise because of hasty actions. So before you commit yourself to doing an act, think. Think twice for easier or simple alternatives that lead to the same desired result. Always choose the simplicity. You will have more peace with simplicity.

Simplicity is about subtracting the obvious and adding the meaningful. How do you get rid of all your stuff that means so much and evokes so much emotion? The simplest way to achieve simplicity is through thoughtful reduction.

Enjoy keeping things simple. The simpler it is, the more you will thrive.

As you simplify, you will notice the most important things are left. A bunch of stuff. This applies to everyday items, closets, and even many of your sentimental treasures. Oftentimes the most difficult stuff to get rid of is all the stuff soaked in great memories. When you become attached to things that remind you of your past and your loved ones, these usually fill you with lovely memories. Because you choose to simplify your life from stuff, these treasures are buried in boxes in the garage or attic. They are only rediscovered during a move or a special trip down memory lane.

After a recent move I experienced, I realized there were several ways to simplify all these sentimental items. I started focusing on what was most important to me, and I began to honor some of my history. I placed some of my items on display or started using them. The remaining items, I gave away to other family members or donated to charity.

When you come across things that you are unable to use, simply let go of them. Someone else may find your sentimental items to be quite useful. Use them or pass them on. I started to give away many of my items to others who could use what I had. I also realized there are many people in need of the many items I had, so I donated them. One of my friends, Bobby Shirley, said to me, "One man's trash is another man's treasure." I looked at my items as good items, so I decided to share them with others who would embrace them. I actually became excited to see how someone else would enjoy an item I had given away. I felt a strong sense of enjoyment and simple release.

As you simplify your life, you will come to the realization that the most sentimental things are more than things. They are stories of the people and places you love and about how you spent your time. Write about the things you love instead of holding onto them. Start a family blog or keep a personal journal. Your words may start out describing your grandparents' items and how they were received; your description may turn into a beautiful story about an afternoon the two of you spent together.

Approach each area, and enjoy what unfolds. Clearly identify what is most meaningful to you. Instead of filling boxes with the things that define your life, spend more time creating your life, giving to others, and sharing your story with thoughts, actions, and gratitude.

To keep things simple, regularly ask yourself this question: "Is this making my life easier and simpler?" Creating simplicity in your life will create a much more focused, powerful, and fun life. Reclaim your fun and playful side. Enjoy and simplify your life.

What do you have in your life that you may reduce out of your life right now to make your life simpler?

Sometimes we don't always get what we deserve. But we do get grace.

A good friend of mine came from an exceptionally broken and destructive family. We had a similar testimony and immediately clicked—a family whose experience included prison, abuse, and drugs. At sixteen years old, she cried in anger to her mentor, "This is not fair! I don't deserve this family, this life!"

Most of us would agree with this outcry from a sweet teenage girl subjected to such a life. Her mentor knew Jesus, and replied, "You're right. You don't deserve this life. You deserve hell and death, and so do I. God's gracious love for us provided a Savior who took our sins and died for them. He didn't deserve death, and we don't deserve life. It is God's grace that we have life at all."

And with that simple word God moved on my dear friend's perspective from disappointment to hope. Her view of her life shifted from anger to gratitude. She found freedom from the bitterness that was beginning to mark her life. Today, she is one of the most joyful and encouraging people I know.

> [1] Have mercy upon me, O God, according to Your lovingkindness; according to the multitude of your tender mercies blot out my transgressions. [2] Wash me thoroughly from my iniquity, and cleanse me from my sin. [3] For I acknowledge my transgressions: and my sin is always before me.
>
> (Psalm 51:1-3)

I want to tell you a story of a woman with *Courage*. I love biblical stories of strength. It helps you envision the biblical heroes back in the day. Her name was Esther. In the year 482 B.C, during the Babylonian captivity of the Jews, a young and beautiful Jewess named Esther stood talking excitedly with her cousin Mordecai, who had given her a home after the death of her mother and father.

"This is a golden opportunity for you, Esther. The king has disposed of his queen, Vashti, for refusing to be put on display along with his other royal possessions, and now all the beautiful women are being called together to be presented to him. From these assembled maidens Xerxes/Ahasuerus will choose a new queen. You can be that queen, Esther!"

"I will obey you, my cousin, as I have always done – but I admire Queen Vashti for remaining a queen in her show of courage. The idea of the king's asking her to do such a thing!"

Esther was not having it. She was not going to be some Kings arm candy. I am totally feeling Esther right now. Esther took her place in line with all the other pretty girls presented by their families all hoping their daughter would be picked so they would no longer be poor. It was at the palace to Hege, the eunuch in charge of the king's women. During the entire year in which the young applicants of women were beautified with myrrh oils and balms and perfumes before being presented before the king, Esther grew in favor of this Hege guy whom she obeyed willingly as she always obeyed her cousin, Mordecai.

Not a day passed when Mordecai was not trying to marry her off. I mean this cousin was anxious, checking on her progress, warning her to keep her Jewish blood a secret. When at last the evening came when Esther was led before the king to spend her night alone with him, she was flushed and more beautiful than ever with excitement. The splendor of the pagan court stretched before the devout Jewish girl in a dancing blur, having a blast, she wasn't there to get married, and she was there to have fun. She was wearing a black dress, dancing on white marble, alabaster, linens, and purple draperies caught with silver rings, gold and silver couches, think Miami penthouse. The king liked his lavish lifestyle but he was very intrigued with Esther. She had definitely caught the Kings eye. Everyone who knew her loved her, and in no time they were married with the confidence of the palace officials and servants.

She soon discovered that her people, the Jews, had a dangerous enemy in her husband's favorite official, Haman. Haman was smart, ruthless, ambitious, and ancient Hitlerian type who would stop at nothing to promote himself. When Mordecai learned of Haman's new decree that all Jews must bow to anyone but the Lord God, he became Haman's most hated enemy.

Using his influence with the king, who cared more for pleasure than for his duties as a ruler at the time of Persia, Haman manipulated a royal decree that all Jews – men, woman and children – would be killed. Mordecai went at once to Queen

Esther, urging her to appear before the king herself and plead for her people.

Queen Esther told her cousin, "Go and gather all the Jews who are available and fast for me; do not eat or drink for three days, night and day. I, too and my maids will similarly fast as well. Then, in spite of the injunction that no one enters without being called, I will go to the king." She lifted her head almost imperceptibly. She did it with an attitude if I die, I die.

The name of the Lord God is not mentioned once in this entire Chapter of Esther in the Bible but He is seen in constant action in almost every fast-moving development in the story of the God freeing the queen of the King of Persia. We must keep in mind now that these ancients were very primitive people, they were a little cray-cray by our standards. Now that Christ has come, much of their behavior we could question. Even her cousin Mordecai's urging Esther to keep her Jewish blood a secret so that she might trick the king into choosing her could be called less than God's best. But as He has always done God was working in the mainstream of human history using as much of human nature as possible in order to keep His plan moving. These Israelite's, scatted into a pagan land from their Holy City of Jerusalem by Nebuchadnezzar, had to be protected. With this in mind, undoubtedly, Esther went into Xerxes' Kingdom, as her cousin said, "For a little time like this." From the remnant of this once powerful Hebrew nation, Gods Son would come. Jehovah worked to preserve this remnant through any human means at hand. Despite their lack of understanding of certain of His higher ways, he knew Esther and her cousin to be devout believers in the Most High. And so, He chose this woman, Esther, to use her influence with a pagan king who did not believe in Him.

God worked with Esther and only through her as on He knew her to be. To her inherent courage He added His own and Esther's good mind was made up. "I will go to the king, and if die, I die." Women then and today are being called upon the Lord God to show this kind of courage. Not in such glamorous surroundings or in such exciting look at me circumstances; but called upon by God to show their maximum courage. And now, as then, He is always willing to add to our inherent courage, His own.

Also, a Woman of Cunning

Three days after her meeting with her cousin, Queen Esther, dressed in royal purple, her head covered in gold and jewels, walked uninvited into the inner Court facing the royal hall where her husband, the king, sat on his high, ornate over the top chair. You could imagine he was annoyed. How he had been foolishly occupied with other matters and so neglected his beautiful Queen Esther? He had not seen her in thirty days at this point. Holding the scepter in his hand outstretched, as Esther walked close enough to touch its golden tip, the king spoke to her intently: "What is on your mind, Queen Esther? What is your wish? It will be granted to you, if it were half the Kingdom." The sensuous king reached toward her, now smiling. Esther moved no closer, but replied beguilingly, "If it pleases your majesty, let the king and Haman attend the banquet I have prepared for the king."

Xerxes ordered for Haman at once. She was relieved and delighted that her request was granted. They were going to the banquet. As Xerxes and Haman were drinking their wine at Esther's banquet, the king grew mellow and attentive. The king asks his wife Esther, "Now tell me, what is your wish? You must have more than he and Haman would attend still a second banquet the next day." Haman went home that night, swollen with pride, convinced he was making headway, not only with the king, but with his queen as well. His wife and his friends bolstered his ego with more praise, but suddenly Haman's face darkened. "Yet all this remains unsatisfactory to me, so long as I see Esther's cousin the Jew seated in the royal gate." "Then stop being so backward my husband," his wife Zaresh said sharply. "Have a gallows erected eighty feet high, and tell the king the first thing in the morning that Mordecai should be hanged on it!" The woman laughed, "Then you can happily accompany the king to the queen's banquet with nothing to ruin your pleasure." The idea interested Haman and he ordered a g scatted allows constructed at once.

Gods hand is seen at work once more that night. Xerxes, the king, could not sleep, and he ordered his record book of memorable events brought out so that he could read away his hours that night. In it he found the detailed account of an almost forgotten event, which happened soon after Esther became his queen. Since she was so much in his thoughts that night, he had read it carefully and remembered well that Mordecai, through a message sent to the king by Esther, had saved his life when two of his door keeping eunuchs had planned to assassinate him. "What honor of distinction has been given to Mordecai for this deed?" The courtiers sitting up in attendance on the sleepless king realized he could still save her. Well, Haman couldn't sleep either that night because he was so mad. Haman came to the idea that why wait until the morning. He came to the king to suggest the execution of Mordecai on the already build gallows.

Xerxes looked curiously at Haman, I am assuming with an expression of 'have you lost your mind man.' The nerve of that guy to wake the king up. The king pretty much asked Haman, "What should be done for a man the king is glad to honor for a great deed?" The king had a suspicion of him and it was evident to everyone but Haman himself. Human was too blind to see because he was blinded by his own greed and was filled with hate. We could only imagine Haman's response, rolling his eyes, and being all dramatic. If you did, you were correct. Haman danced around the king describing just the kind of royal honor he felt was surely about to be his own. He would give the man one of the king's robes and a horse. The king thought it was a great idea. He told Haman to get a robe and a horse and give it to Mordecai, the Jew who was sitting at the royal gate. Haman was hot to trot. But he could not disobey the king's orders. He thought it was all going to him. Haman was forced to carry out the kings command himself to honor Mordecai, and then to go in shame by himself to Esther's banquet. When the men were once more drinking their wine, the king again asked Esther's pleasure. Once more he offered half his kingdom to her. But Esther asked that if the king would grant her wish and let her people go. The king was like hold up, "Your people?" She responded and told him her people who have been sold, and I and my people! She went steadily laying it thick for her king, admitting her Jewish blood to him for the first time. You authorized the selling of my people, and then to be destroyed and then killed to be obliterated. I am begging you for our lives, my king my husband! I could only imagine her fear. As the story goes the king stood up, "Who is the man who dared contemplate such a thing?" She tells him an enemy, a wicked man named Haman.

Haman covered probably in utter terror, was like um, yup I'm busted, probably my que to leave, trying to avoid the Kings fury. And in the foolish desperate man he was, when the king went out to the garden to cool off and hit the reset button, Haman attempted to hit on the king's wife pleading for his life, which now is in Esther's hand, a Jewish woman. The king caught him in his act of boldness with Esther and what Haman might have hoped was going to save his life brought it out to an immediate end. He was hung at once on the gallows he had built. Esther had been sent for just this time, and although His name is not mentioned in the biblical account, God had been with her to honor her courage and her wit.

Point of this story was to share with you not only was she a total babe of the Bible, she was a woman of courage, and she was a woman of great wit. Her first appearance before the king was a risky one – here, she had needed only of her courage. But after the king ended up liking her and marrying her, she put her excellent mind to work. She did not plunge to her knees begging for the lives of her people to be spared that first day. But set up two big dinners with Haman, knowing darn and well, her enemy, would be her guest. She flattered Haman, knowing he would trip himself in his own issues and try to have her cousin killed. But he did trip, all the way to the gallows.

She did not fall into Haman's trap, which sometimes us women allow are emotions to rule our every movement and reaction. Esther used her level head, even though her heart was heavy with fear for her own life as Jewess, and for the lives of her people. Jesus said we are to be gentle as Doves but as wise as serpents. Esther was both. The combination worked. We are told in James' that when we are in need of wisdom beyond our own, God will supply it. I like the fact that James bothered to add that God would not belittle us for asking. Why should He? God knows more clearly than we know that we are all faced with situations and painful moments that require wisdom beyond our innate ability. God supplied Esther with His wisdom in the hard places, just as He is eager to supply us in our times of need.

He cannot do this, however, if we are plunging around feeling sorry for ourselves, blinded by our emotional prison, as Haman was. Haman was fueled by his emotions and issues. Any woman, who knows God, has access to His wisdom at any time, under any circumstance; her part is to keep her emotions in check. Kick out those thoughts of shame, guilt, insecurity, anxiety and stress, and you will be open to receive His wisdom, guidance, vision and direction. You are courageous just like Esther. And God is just as eager to give you the wisdom as he did Esther.

Say this prayer for courage:

> [1] Keep me safe, my God, for in you I take refuge. [2] I say to the LORD, "You are my Lord; apart from you I have no good thing."

> (Psalm 16:1-2)

There are many days where I feel an overwhelming sense of discouragement, exhaustion, or frustration. It might be little things that bring about these feelings in me, or it might be major life events that have left me weary and hurting, but either way, I know I don't have the strength on my own to make it through. Its days like those where I find prayers like this comforting. When we feel those feelings creeping in, may we instead choose to kneel before our Father in heaven and ask him for the strength and courage we need to carry on.

We often don't think about the connection between prayer and courage. But prayer is how we remind ourselves of what God has done in the past and who he is. He is infinitely good, wise, strong, loving, and perfect. And that infinite wisdom, goodness, love and perfection is what he uses to care for us every day. When we look back on our lives, we can see how all God has promised is true – he has never left us alone in our problems. He is always with us, always providing for our needs, always loving, carrying and strengthening us each day for the challenges ahead. When we take time to pray a prayer of gratitude for what God has done, it will encourage us to pray boldly for the help we need in the present and future moments to come.

> [6] Do not be anxious about anything, but in every situation, by prayer and petition, with thanksgiving, present your requests to God. [7] And the peace of God, which transcends all understanding, will guard your hearts and your minds in Christ Jesus.
>
> (Philippians 4:6-7). Amen.

CHAPTER 11

Unlike Before

A Contended mind is the greatest blessing a man
can enjoy in this world.

– Joseph Addison

ONE OF THE WONDERFUL THINGS ABOUT GOD IS THAT
He loves new beginnings. With God, you don't have to live in the
bondage and pain of yesterday; you can live in the beauty and
promise of tomorrow. That's why scripture promises that Gods
compassion and mercies are "new every morning" (Lamentations
3:23). God doesn't just allow "do-overs;" He created them!
Consider the stories we read about in the Bible.

- Moses killed an Egyptian and ran from his destiny
  but God gave him a new beginning as the deliverer of
  His people.

- David was a Shepard boy who was slighted by his own
  father but God gave him a new beginning as the king
  of Israel.

- Gideon was afraid of the enemy and hiding in a wine press but God gave him a new beginning as a mighty military leader.

So, do you believe me now when I tell you no matter what the personal struggle or failure, God forgives, heals, restores, and makes things new? He's been doing it since man first sinned, so long before you honey! And he is still doing it today Thank God for that or we would be in trouble! You know what else; God wants to give you a new start. **Regardless of the past, pain, pressure, trauma, anxiety, or stress you've been living with, God wants to give you a brand-new start.** He wants to take all that away and give you a new freedom in Him.

In 2 Corinthians 5:17 you will read this promise stated as follows:

Therefore if any person is [ingrafted] in Christ (The Messiah) he is a new creation (a new creation altogether); the old [previous moral and spiritual condition] has passed away. Behold the fresh and new has come!

I don't know about you, but that is fantastic news – the fresh and new has come! Stress, anxiety, worry and pressure are the old things that you had learned to live with but God is making all things new. You don't have to live that way anymore. Today, tomorrow, and every day forward can be a new start. You can live full of peace and overflowing with joy. Today isn't just another day when you are stressed out and overwhelmed – today can be the first day of the rest of your new life!

Listen there are going to be times when those stupid old stresses and anxieties try to come knocking on your door. "Ding Dong. Can I come in?" Nope because God is making all things no, bye Felicia! You have learned in this book how to kick them out but that doesn't mean they won't try to sneak back in. So in this last chapter, I want to give you some final tools for your spiritual library that will help you live a peaceful, joy-filled life from this day forward. Choosing to live with joy doesn't mean that we never experience any negative emotions like anger, sadness, or disappointment. Believe me your spouse will still aggravate you, some days him just existing will do that, but I did not choose your spouse for you that is a whole separate issue.

Anyways sorry not really, therapy works, okay I'm kidding, but we love our marriage counselor. Okay It does mean that we have a choice not to let those emotions rule us. You can visit but you can't stay here. Most of the emotions that we experience in life are very normal and even necessary. How could I be qualified to minister to you about your emotions if I had never experienced anything but good ones? All of our experiences in life are what form us into the people that we are. But once again, I want to stress that we can choose to let our emotions rule our behavior or to manage them in such a way that, although we don't deny their existence, we do deny them the right to control us.

I made a hair appointment one day at a salon, my normal salon stylist was full that day, and my emotions were flying. I had very long hair at the time. I can imagine you're wondering like Aimee what the heck you have a five month old what are you thinking having all that time to devote to your long locks of hair? I wasn't. You're right. I was struggling my old anxieties and my old stupid issues were knocking at my door and kept ringing the door like an unwelcomed kid that wouldn't go away. I mean that in the most humorous way. My son goes to his fathers every other weekend and they always seem to ring the door and knock when he is not there, and I am trying to take nap. I find it pretty humorous.

I was eating some Hagen Diaz – chocolate flavor that is the best and my favorite and my daughters favorite. Kidding, I only give her like one bite. I had a vision, I don't have enough ice-cream, and I really hate washing my hair, I never have enjoyed it. If you know me you would know I have an absurd amount of dry shampoo, my thighs disagree because my thighs right now are the only thing not social distancing ok! I said to myself, "I am going to cut my hair. I need to cut out all those things that don't matter, that I don't have time for and cut them out of your life honey like an ex." (Yes, I actually talk to myself like that in my head.) In my mind, I am basically a Kardashian distant cousin ha! Kidding no relation. So, I got ready for my appointment, which was at 2:00 p.m. that day.

I brought up the ice cream because I had just finished twenty-one days of fasting and prayer. I had done many fasts but this one I stuck the closest to, and it was the most spiritual experience I had ever had. Mentally, physically, spiritually everything was so clear. It was like wearing lens of clarity. Every issue, every struggle I was having became sharp. I was able to slow down enough to see it ALL clearly, and cut it out. But I did not cut out Hagen Diaz that was something I was not willing to part with. A year had just gone by. It was the first year I had lived without my mother. I was gaining weight, feeding my issues, and emotionally I was just exhausted, so it was time for a haircut. It was my redemption year, my year that I cleaned the house and journeyed to emotional freedom.

That weekend we went to church like normal. My church has an amazing worship team; we like to attend earlier service because I become very hungry at late service. I almost chewed my husband's arm off last time. I think after that he packed me snacks, he is thoughtful that way. Our favorite worship song came on and it was the second time in my whole life that I have ever smelled incense.

I remember tapping my husband on the shoulder because he is way taller than me, and I asked him "Do you smell that?"

He responded, "No," but I said, "Honey, it smells like incense burning."

He said, "Sweetie, that's the Holy Spirit." It gave me goosebumps. No one was sitting around us, no one's perfume I would have mistaken that for.

I ended up feeling a little sassy at the hair salon; I was feeling thankful that God had given me that vision over my life. I ended up cutting twelve inches off and donating it. I felt great like I had one less thing to worry about now. It was a very feminine, invigorating feeling for me. I even felt cool enough to take a selfie and #Shorthairdontcare and #Shortandsassy.

Choose your newfound freedom and live with hope.

How do you generally feel about your future? Do you have hope that good things will happen? Or do you generally feel stressed, expecting negative or disappointing things to happen? I grew up in a very negative house; I lived in an abusive atmosphere with negative people, alcoholism, fear and anger. Then was married in a domestic violence relationship. I developed an attitude that it was better to expect nothing good than to expect something good and be disappointed when it didn't happen. Sadly, I often wondered, what's going to go wrong next?

It wasn't until I was an adult that I realized I was living with negative expectations, which created a vague feeling around me all the time that something bad was going to happen. Then one day, God spoke to me, you have to right size your expectations. He showed me that I was dreading that something bad was going to happen, but He wanted me to expect good things to happen. Jeremiah 29:11 tells us that Gods thoughts and plans for us are "for welfare and pace and not for evil, to give you hope in your final outcome." God wanted me to be joyful, believe and even yell aloud, "Something Good is coming!"

"Better is the end than the beginning." (Ecclesiastes 7:8). You may have had a rough start, but you don't have to have a rough finish. Don't keep dwelling on the negative. God is saying in the scripture, "Something better is coming!" and that's what God was speaking to me. He wants you to do that also. Expecting good and living with a positive attitude are great stress relievers. God is good all the time, and as we walk with Him and learn his ways, we can expect more and more good things to come to us and flow through us to other hurting people. Negative expectation always equals pressure and that means stress. The truth is God doesn't work in us through negative attitudes of any kind. Whether it is worry, anxiety, self-pity, jealousy, laziness, or un-forgiveness – these are not peace-producing attitudes. God works through faith! But in order to have faith, it is essential that we first have hope. Faith and hope go together – you can't have on without the other. Hope is a favorable and confident expectation; it's an expectant attitude that something good is going to happen and things will work out, no matter what situation we're facing.

Zechariah 9:12 says:

> Return to the stronghold, you prisoners of hope;
> even today do I declare that I will restore double your
> former prosperity to you.

I really like the phrase 'prisoners of hope.' Think about it: If you're a prisoner of hope, you have no choice about it – you can't be negative. And when times are tough and you're dealing with disappointment or you're feeling stress creep in, hope will cause you to rise up in faith and say, "God, I praise you and I believe you're working on this situation and working in me. My faith, trust, and hope are in you!" Believe that God is working, and avoid thinking that God will work at some time in the future. Faith is always "now," and it is what we believe now that affects the life we are living now!

When you have a positive mindset, you can't be defeated!

Hope is determined to see Gods best, and it never gives up. God wants us to expectantly trust that He can change what needs to be changed, that we can accomplish what He has called us to do, and that His promises are going to come true in our lives. If we will be steadfast in our hope, we can't lose – we are destined to succeed with Gods help. I can tell you for sure that our enemy, Satan, is always working overtime to steal hope from us. He is the source of all the temptation we experience to be hopeless, anxious, and stressed out in our life. But the truth is that we already have victory as long as we apply Gods principals to our lives trusting in Him at ALL times.

There will be tough days. Don't assume that everything will get better the minute you put this book down. We are impatient. Human nature is now in an Amazon Prime next day delivery impatient. We like things quickly, well most things. Why is it that although it takes us years to get into our messes, we expect God to get us out of them in a few days? In John 16:33, Jesus tells us that we are going to have tribulation, trials, distress, and frustration in the world, but in spite of that, we can be of good cheer and take heart. Why? Because He has overcome the world. And when we live in Him, we become overcomers, too! That's why Jesus died for us. He came to save us from sin and death and to give us an abundant life – now.

I am determined to have everything Jesus died to give me. I encourage you to take that same decision – be determined to receive and enjoy every good thing Jesus died to give you. You'll have to do it on purpose. But you can be determined to do what God wants you to do and refuse to live with negative expectations. Ask God to help you live in hope and declare by faith, "Something good is going to happen to me!"

Keep pressing, keep sowing

There are four things you can do for spiritual growth. Know God, find your freedom, discover your purpose, and make a difference. The gift of healing is the divine strength or ability to act as an intermediary in faith and prayer, and by the laying-on hands for the healing of physical, emotional and mental illnesses. Have faith, it is a measure of trust in the Holy Spirits power. You know what I used to write on the bathroom mirror wall in lipstick, after God saved me when I was a broken and reckless on the shower floor? "The happiest person is the prettiest." It didn't have to do with looks; it had to do with how I felt. It had to do with *unlike before.*

Unlike the past when I was living in an emotional prison of shame, it was unlike before when I didn't have spiritual freedom.

I was about being truly happy. It was finding my purpose and trusting God and stop living in a box. I had to decrease so I could increase with a positive attitude towards life. Living a happy life is kind of like marriage; sometimes in a marriage to love is a choice – you have to work at it every day, just like being happy. Did you know there are more than five thousand songs on the radio about home played every hour? That's why it is so important to be happy. To have a happy home. If you were to ask most people, they would want their family to be happy. Bring to Him daily your praises not just when your struggling or in trouble.

An important part of battling stress and worry is making right choices while you are hurting, discouraged, frustrated, confused, or under pressure – even though the right choice is often the harder choice. When you're in the middle of terrible stress you naturally want to take the path of least resistance. Those are the very moments when you can make a conscious effort to make the tougher choice. To reap right results in life, you must decide to do the right thing when you don't feel like it. I call it keep pressing keep sowing – and knowing how to do it is one of the most important components of being a person who doesn't live as a victim of your pain.

Any kind of progress in life requires effort. Being a person who makes major life changes will require an investment on your part. You'll only get to where you want to be by willingly sacrificing and pushing through the obstacles or adversities that stand in your way. But you can be assured that sacrifice always eventually brings a reward. Your obstacle might be a habit of giving in to stressful situations – in the past you may have simply lived as a victim of your environment allowing the circumstances in your life to determine your mood. Whatever it may be, you are the only one who can press through it; no one else can do that for you. I believe it is time to take back your life, and stare those fears dead in the face and follow Gods will instead of bowing down to pressure that is designed to prevent you from living your destiny and calling on your life.

Maybe you have tried to make some changes in the past. Perhaps you tried to the point that you are now weary, exhausted, or discouraged. Maybe you don't see a way out of your situation. If so, then you are at the precise point where you need to summon fresh strength from God and press in and sow on one more time. Many times, we grow tired and we are faltering in our determination, if we do not continually lean on God trusting in His strength rather than our own strength. We can make the decision to press through with grit but we never experience success in anything unless we rely on God to help us. His grace is always sufficient to enable our spiritual freedom and find our purpose to focus on what we need to do.

When we put our hope and dependence in God, He'll give us the strength we need and an open heart to heal. Don't wait to feel the strength before you step up and step out to be all that God called you to be. You are a babe; you are strong, fearless, bold and confident. You have everything you need to walk in boldness right now. God is the God of "now." Keep moving forward, even when it gets really hard. Believe me, I could have given up so many times. God will always show up and show out and do what we could not do on our own.

> But those who hope in the Lord will renew their strength. They will soar on wings like eagles; they will run and not grow weary, they will walk and not be faint.
>
> (Isaiah 40:31)

Girl, look how far you have come!

Let me tell you about a conversation I had with a friend of mine we'll call her "Sally." Sally told me, "Aimee, I have been a Christian for over ten years now and I'm just not getting anywhere. I'm as weak as I was when I first accepted Jesus in my heart and I still fail. I just don't know if it's worth it." She was very discouraged and very hard on herself and tears kept running down her checks as she talked about her mistakes and past choices.

She went on to say, "By now I know all the right things to do, but I still don't do them. I even deliberately do something mean-spirited or unkind. What kind of Christian am I?"

You probably know a few people like this.

I answered her very quickly and matter of fact, "Probably a growing Christian! If you weren't growing, you wouldn't be sad about your failures. The fact that you're upset means you care. You would be satisfied about your spiritual level and not concerned with growing."

She said, "But Aimee, I still fail so often!"

I went on to tell Sally she was correct that she had failed. But all of us do. We are really good at screwing things up sometimes. None of us are perfect. If we are not careful, we can focus only on what we haven't accomplished and where we have been weak and never see the progress we have made. You are making progress, sometimes we have to get out of our way. When you focus on the progress you haven't made its easy to feel bad and want to give up. That's not the way God works. No matter how many mistakes we make, God doesn't give up on us and He is not going to give up on you my dear! The spirit continues to work with us and makes us more like Christ. Remember, we were created in His image. My advice to you and my friend Sally, and to all Christians, and women who face trauma and are trying to overcome their pain, is to look at all God has done in your life rather than seeing all that's left still to do. Yes, life is sometimes a pain in the rear, and there are times when we fail and make mistakes. We don't ever reach the place where we never struggle or never give into temptation. But here is the key thing to remember: God sent Jesus because we are weak at times and we need His help and forgiveness. Jesus is not only with you, but He is also for you. **He knows your heart's desire is to do better. He knows where you came from, but He also knows where you are headed and He will never give up on you.**

Never stop fighting.

"Let us not become weary in doing good, for at the proper time we will reap a harvest if we do not give up."

(Galatians 6:9)

In this scripture, the apostle Paul is simply encouraging us to keep on keeping on! Don't be a quitter! Don't have that old 'I'm just going to give up, it's pointless' attitude. God is looking for strong courageous women who are going to find spiritual freedom and use their story to help other women. Even at times when progress seems slow, remember that any progress is better than going backward. For many years, I felt I was making very little, if any, progress in my spiritual growth and in overcoming bad habits and behaviors. But now as I look back it is amazing to see how different I am from years ago, and the same thing is going on and the same thing is happening and will continue happening to you. I wish I could be there to witness it and cheer you on! Believe me if I can do it, so can you. I am not a Pastor. I have never served in a leadership role at my church. God has put in my vision that He is going to use my testimony to help other women find freedom. I'm not going to lie, I laughed at first, like "Ding Dong, God are you sure you want to use me? Aren't you afraid of what I might say?" I mean after all this entire book is titled *Sassy & Saved*.

Whatever you may be facing or experiencing in your life right now, I want to encourage you to stay the course, and stay positive, show yourself grace, love and compassion. Refuse to go back to those anxious, worried, stressed-filled, trauma lived moments. God is with you. Who can be against you? It is not Gods will for you to live in shame. Jesus came to give us freedom, peace, and we can learn to live happily and love ourselves peacefully amid turmoil and enjoy our lives while God does the fixing. Stay focused on the fullness of who you belong to and who you were called to be. Give the control to Jesus. You are fearfully and wonderfully made. I cannot wait to see what the next Chapter looks like for you!

APPENDIX

Renew and receive the gift of Salvation

Would you like to walk through this season with me? I am here with you. God is not mad at you! He isn't counting your sins and holding them against you. He wants, so much, to have a personal relationship with you that He sent Jesus, His only Son, to shed His blood, die on the cross, and then be raised from the dead. He did all that so that you can be set free from the bondage of sin and the fear of death, and enter into eternal life.

As a sister in Christ, as a friend, as a shoulder to cry on, as a believer we can walk through this life together. You are not alone. I would love to share the Gospel of Jesus with you. What is Salvation? Salvation in Theology is deliverance from sin and its consequences, believed by Christians to be brought about by faith in Christ. God wants you to walk in with wholeness and freedom from the bondage of pain, loss, insecurity, doubt and fear. He has made a way for you through the life, death and resurrection of His Son, Jesus so you can walk in Him.

> Jesus answered, "I am the way and the truth and the life. No one comes to the Father except through me"
>
> (John 14:6 NIV)

"Jesus died and became sin so that we could become the righteousness of God."

(2 Corinthians 5:21)

God laid down his life for you on the cross so that we could be born again. When you confess with your mouth and believe in your heart that Jesus is Lord, not only are we born again, we also receive His Holy Spirit, the promise of our salvation. Everything God is, we have access to it. Everything that held us back from speaking to God face to face is gone. When we turn from our own ways, surrender our lives and ways of thinking and make Jesus Lord and King of our eternal souls, we are reunited into the family of God. Salvation is a gift that Christ paid for us on the cross. It's a gift freely given, nothing we could have done in our own efforts to earn it or deserve it. It's a gift God gives us because he loves us eternally. If you would like to receive the gift of salvation through Jesus' death and resurrection, pray this prayer out loud as you confess with your mouth what you believe in your heart to be true.

9 If you declare with your mouth, "Jesus is Lord," and believe in your heart that God raised him from the dead, you will be saved. 10 For it is with your heart that you believe and are justified, and it is with your mouth that you profess your faith and are saved.

(Romans 10:9-10)

You are good enough, you have a purpose beyond the pain, and you are free.

Say this prayer out loud right now:

> *"Dear God, I want to be a part of your family. You said in Your Word that if I acknowledge that you raised Jesus from the dead, and that I accept Him as my Lord and Savior, I would be saved. So God, I now say that I believe You raised Jesus from the dead and that He is alive and well. I accept Him now as my personal Lord and Savior. I accept my salvation from sin right now. I am now saved. Jesus is my Lord. Jesus is my Savior. Thank you, Father God, for forgiving me, saving me, and giving me eternal life with you. Amen!"*

I wish I could be there to give you a great big hug. Heaven is throwing a celebration for your homecoming. So you received salvation and just prayed a sincere prayer of faith and you're wondering what to do next as a new Christian, check out these helpful suggestions:

- Salvation is by grace, through faith. There's nothing you did, or ever can do, to deserve it. Salvation is a free gift from God. All you have to do is receive it!

- Tell someone about your decision. It's important that you tell someone to make it public, secure, and firm. Find a brother or sister in the Lord and tell him or her, "Hey, I made a decision to follow Jesus." Tell someone today if you can. It's a great way to seal the deal. Baptism.

- Talk to God every day. You don't have to use big fancy words. There are no right and wrong words. Just be yourself. Thank the Lord daily for your salvation. Pray for others in need. Seek his direction. Pray for the Lord to fill you daily with his Holy Spirit. There is no limit to prayer. You can pray with your eyes closed or open, while sitting or standing, kneeling or lying on your bed, anywhere, anytime.

- Find a church and get plugged in somewhere.

- Start with the four essentials to Spiritual Growth. Reading your Bible daily, get plugged in to a small group, meet with other believers, and pray daily.

- Learn the Basics of Christianity.

Once you established the four essentials to spiritual growth you are well on your way. I am so proud of you. If you are interested in more avenues of spiritual growth, you can start doing a Daily Devo, Bible study, studying the Bible and avoiding temptation as that will be a daily requirement. Once you've made these four essential steps a regular part of your Christian life, it won't be long before you're eager to venture even deeper into your relationship with Jesus Christ. But don't feel rushed or get ahead of yourself and God. Remember, you have all eternity to grow in faith. Jesus has everything you need to live in your purpose. You are well on your way, beautiful!

UNQUALIFIED & CALLED

We'd love to have you join us at one of our gatherings. Unqualified and Called in St. Augustine, FL. Please go to www.unqualifiedandcalled.com for more details and information. Unqualified & Called seeks to glorify God through studying the word of Jesus, ministering to the needs of women, and cultivating a spirit of unity. We equip women to live with passion and purpose and to walk in boldness. We activate women to walk in freedom, spiritually, emotionally, and physically, and to see others set free within their society of influence.

ACKNOWLEDGMENTS

TO MY HUSBAND MORGAN, YOU HAVE SEEN ME AND encouraged and pushed me to finding my purpose beyond the pain. Finding Spiritual Freedom. You saw past that stubborn, prideful young me, and finely kept encouraging me to forgive my parents. You showed me what restoration and much healing looked like. Our spiritual inheritance is a beautiful story, and I love walking in redemption with you.

Thank you to my mother who is looking down. You are the spiritual proof of one who fought to the very end for freedom and what was right; you stood up for equality in people. You were a one of a kind woman, and although we had really hard times but in the end, we found healing and restoration. Thank you for giving me that.

To my teenager, for doing the dishes, most of the time lol, when mom was up late working on her book, or bringing me a sandwich, love you dude.

To my younger son, for countless times of peek-a-boo so mommy could finish her book with still hanging on to my sanity.

To COVD-19, for showing my family and me to slow down and enjoy one another, that family is the most important thing, and that my puzzle skills can probably improve.

To my beautiful sisters, each and every one of you. I am beyond blessed to be able to do our wonderful, crazy, messy life together.

All the babies and pets, we are one great big fun family. I love you all deeply.

To my very best friend Mindy, I love your free spirited fun self. You are such an inspiration for women overcoming difficult situations and healing themselves as you yourself have overcome such adversities, and I cannot wait for you to share it with the world. Thank you for always making sure I used there and their correctly; you are my grammar gangster.

Thank you GG, for being the biggest cheerleader to women, and accepting me with wide open arms; you ladies are my bonus sisters!

To my children's teachers, thank you for loving my children as yours. I don't know how you do it; thank you to COVID-19 for showing me that teaching is not my spiritual gift, I will never complain about "Teacher Appreciation Day" ever again, whatever you want it's yours.

To all the women who have inspired me, sown into my life, and paved a way that pushed me countless times forward, so many times I quit counting. There are too many to write it all.

Thank you to everyone on the Book Baby team who helped me so much. You helped create years of just journaling my dream into pages.

To my Father,

Jesus the Healer and companion, thank you for asking me by the hand even when I was kicking and screaming, and walking with me in and through ever season of life. For being faithful, kind, and real, for being the never-ending love that healed all of pain. Thank you for giving me the confidence to write this book with you. This book is yours and wouldn't exist without you. You are actually all I want and need. I love you.

Love,

Your daughter.

ABOUT THE AUTHOR

Born and raised in Florida, a St. Augustine native, Aimee is the Founder of Unqualified & Called. Aimee attended nursing school in St. Augustine and has been a nurse for over nine years, working in hospitals and serving patients and families in their most delicate times. Aimee later went on to gain experience in Marketing & Business Development and founded Miller Legal Nurse Consulting Group, LLC. She serves and attends at her local church. She began her Bible studies at home ministering to her friends and family. She hopes to inspire people from her blogs, books, social media and friendships to spread the love of Jesus one women at a time.

Morgan and Aimee currently live in St. Augustine, Florida and their greatest joy is spending quality family time with their four children: Alex, Brian, Brady and Charlotte. Aimee's heart is out for inspiring women to live with passion, purpose and to walk in boldness.

"I'm passionate about seeing women encounter God in such a personal and vulnerable way. Exposing familiar misconceptions, barriers, and a dull life without God."

– Aimee Miller

Freedom is her passion as she has herself been set free from so much pain due to her love of Jesus. It's one of the biggest reasons why she launched 'Unqualified & Called' in St. Augustine, FL. Currently,

Aimee's life is focused on raising her young family, writing, traveling, and speaking to different churches all around the world.

STAY CONNECTED
WITH THE
AUTHOR

AIMEE P.
MILLER

AIMEEPMILLER.COM
FACEBOOK.COM/AIMEEPMILLER.PAGE
INSTAGRAM @ AIMEEPMILLER

GATHER

EQUIP women to live with passion, purpose and walk in boldness. ACTIVATE women to walk in freedom, spiritually, emotionally, physically and see others set free in their society of influence.

UNQUALIFIEDANDCALLED.COM
@UNQUALIFIEDANDCALLED
#UNQUALIFIEDANDCALLED

ALSO FROM **AIMEE P. MILLER**
COMING JUNE 2021

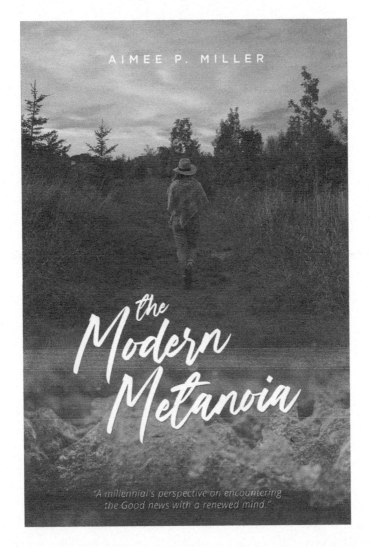

"*The modern Metanoia is a millennials compelling perspective on encountering the Good news. You're a renewed mind away from the adventure of your life.*"